The Power of Full Awareness

Live with a Purpose, Driven with Potential

Tasha M. Gooden

1

Legal Notice and Disclaimer:

Any trademarks, service marks, product names or named features are assumed to be the property of their respective owners and are used only for reference. There is no implied endorsement if we use one of these terms.

Finally, use your head. Nothing in this Guide is intended to replace common sense, legal, medical or other professional advice and is meant to inform and entertain the reader. So, have fun and get your life back.

Library of Congress

Sentiments of the Heart

ISBN: 9798698619789ISBN

Printed in the United States of America

Contents

Introduction

Eighty-six thousand four hundred seconds -- for the reason in time ℮

We have all heard the expression, "You are living on borrowed time." Of course, this means to go on living after the time you should have died. The phrase goes back to the seventeenth century. My sister was given several weeks to live after being diagnosed with inoperable brain cancer. She went on to live for five more years and even survived one round of hospice care to live a few more years after that. She just did not want to die. She lived many happy, if not healthy, years on borrowed time. I often wondered who she paid this time back to and who she borrowed it from. I think if you live life like there will be no tomorrow you are living on borrowed time. We all know people who disproportionately flaunt the risks of life. People who drink and drive are living on borrowed time. People who ride motorcycles without wearing a helmet are living on borrowed time. People who do not exercise or watch their weight are living on borrowed time. People who smoke are living on borrowed time. Each day you take unnecessary risks, you are living on borrowed time. You may cheat death each day, but it is also a day that you owe to someone and you will eventually be called upon to pay. The actuaries are betting millions that you will die when they say you will and people living on borrowed time generally pay up when due.

Are you one of the people living on borrowed time? What is the cost you pay for living on borrowed time? Who do you borrow this time from? Who do you pay it back to? When do you think they will come to collect? I think you borrow it from those who love and those who care for you. They would rather have you than the money.

Introduction

Dear reader,

The best dream happens when you are awake. It wasn't until we were broken that we began to see the light of life. We can all change; you don't have to be a leader in position to positively influence others.

Being positive is self-fulfilling, contagious and a positive influence in the lives of others. A commitment to be our best and to inspire others to be their best sets up a legacy that motivates others to respond and it is a byproduct of having and demonstrating the right attitudes. The timeless characteristics of honesty, integrity and accountability are what inspire people to trust and follow righteousness.

This approach is effective. We share our philosophy on how to improve your attitude and your ability to positively impact your life and those in your circle of friends. The ideas you are about to read are timeless and universal. You can apply them daily in life. Why is this worth reading? Good question. We know you're busy. So, we've done our best to fill this book with insightful, practical, and motivating insights you can apply immediately in a workbook format.

This book has a ring of truth. In order to understand this book, you need to know that my ideas are not abstract concepts or esoteric, academic theology conjured up by an author who has no real-life experience. This information is about transformation, and it is meant to be shared.

Our attitude transcends what we believe. There is no special difference in a positive attitude that inspires change. You cannot change until you change. Your breakthrough will not happen in a day. You will need to embrace it in love and commitment with continuous improvement in the process. It will require a change in your thinking.

You will have to be patient, kind and walk in love and understanding to yourself. You cannot be jealous, conceited and proud in your thinking. You cannot be ill mannered, selfish, or irritable. You cannot keep a record of wrong things. You will have to be proactive not reactive; you cannot rejoice in evil but be happy with truth, honesty and integrity. You will need to remain steadfast, focused and committed to the vision.

Tasha M.
Gooden

ACKNOWLEDGEMENTS

There are many people who invested in the development of this project, who must be and should be acknowledged. Without them this would not have been able to meet the stringent obstacles of our lives and provide some clarity and quality of information that is essential to this kind of project. I am honored and extremely grateful to have the support of many; you were my inspiration through many trials and tribulations.

To my family and close friends: your indirect/direct input helped in shaping me, and I would not have made it this far without you all.

Thank you for your tireless labor to enhance my life with insights and creativity. You all helped with great significance to the components in this endeavor to complete this project. You all inserted your enthusiasm, encouragement, wisdom and your belief in my message to the world.

You were to be in my life…that I may be in the lives of others and share my story.

A special thanks to my husband Charles L. Gooden. Your support and ability to give without looking for anything in return makes it easy to love you.

Thank you!

Self-Management
Proverbs 18:21

Managing who we are and the energy that moves us is the key to enduring. It is also the key to total health, well-being, happiness, and life balance. There are 86,400 seconds in a day, and it's fixed. However, the quantity and quality of energy within us is not. Our energy is in a constant state of release. What we do with that energy during those fixed hours in the day makes all the difference.

The principal approach to management

- Full engagement requires calling on four separate but related sources of energy:
    - Mental Energy
    - Emotional Energy
    - Physical Energy
    - Spiritual Energy
- You must balance energy expenditure with intermittent energy renewal.
- To build your energy capacity, you must push beyond your normal limits, training in the same systematic way as elite athletes.

Incorporating positive energy routines for managing energy are the key to full engagement and sustained high performance. Rituals have power. They insure you use as little conscious energy as possible to only use it where it is most needed. If used properly and with purpose, rituals will free you to strategically focus your energy in more creative and enriching ways.

- Creating positive rituals is the most powerful means for you, the author of your life, to effectively manage your energy in the service of full engagement. By doing so, it allows you to become all that you have been intended to become.

You must sustain healthy oscillatory rhythms at four levels for optimal balance. These four levels, *mental, emotional, physical, and spiritual,* are the foundation of the "**Performance Pyramid**."

Mental Awareness

Mental health includes our emotional, psychological, and social well-being. It affects how we think, feel, and act. It also helps determine how we handle stress, relate to others, and make choices. Mental health is important at every stage of life, from childhood and adolescence through adulthood. Over the course of your life, if you experience mental health problems your thinking, mood, and behavior could be affected. Many factors contribute to mental health problems, and associated factors, exercise and activity levels, smoking, Diet, Physical health, Abuse, Social and Community Activities, Relationship, Meditation and other Relaxation Techniques, and Healthy Sleep,

Positive mental health allows people to:

- Realize their full potential.
- Cope with the stresses of life.
- Work productively.
- Make meaningful contributions to their communities.

Emotional Awareness

- Value yourself. Treat yourself with kindness and respect. Avoid self-criticism.

- Take care of your body. Taking care of yourself physically can improve your mental health.

- Surround yourself with good people.

- Give of yourself.

- Learn how to deal with stress.

- Quiet your mind.

- Set realistic goals.

- Break up the monotony.

Physical Awareness

- The two critical functions of your makeup are breathing and eating. These are regulated by the things you eat and breathe the quality of your sleep, the degree to which you get intermittent recovery during your day and your level of fitness.
- The power of controlled breathing is a powerful tool for self-regulation. It is a means to relax and tap into the energy trapped inside you. Once you tap into your internal energy, your external energy will help you identify what you're becoming physically. This not only quiets the body, but also your mind and emotions.
- For example, I discovered my eating patterns helped to contribute to my overall ability to discover who I am and how it impacts those around me. Maintaining sustained energy required eating healthy. Unhealthy living will lead to a downward spiral in our overall health, spirituality, and physical well-being.

Spiritual Awareness

- Be quiet.
- Be open.
- Practice being non-judgmental and having an open mind.
- Be receptive to pain or times of sorrow.
- Practice forgiveness.
- Pray, meditate and worship.
- Live joyfully.
- Allow yourself to believe in things that aren't easily explainable.

Enduring the Change

- <u>Goal</u> – Who do I want to become? What do I want to achieve? What is my ultimate goal?
- <u>Define Purpose</u> - How should I spend my 86/4 in a way that is consistent with my deepest values?
- <u>Face the truth</u> – How are you spending your time/energy now?

- <u>Take Action</u> – Close the gap between whom you

  are and who you want to become.

In order for you to make a change that is lasting, you must build serial rituals focusing on one element at a time. This helps you build the foundation necessary to reach your goal.

The boot camp exercise

There are two shifts that change and increase the likelihood of successful paradigm change – a shift in your attitudes and in your emotional well-being. It's a physical and mental boot camp training exercise. Through the exercise, you learn what you don't know that's in you to face the challenges before you.

<u>Situational Awareness</u>

<u>Chart the course</u> - Start each day by revisiting your

vision. Identify what you intend to accomplish and

how you will conduct yourself along the way.

Incorporated in your journal

<u>Chart the progress</u> – Hold yourself accountable at the end of each day. **"The beginning of your day and the ending of your day is a reflection of what you see in the mirror."** Accountability demands that you face the truth. Defining a desired outcome and holding yourself accountable each day gives focus and direction to your life and pushes you toward building your total being. It is both protection against your infinite capacity for self–deception and a source of information. Opening your awareness and tapping into the true source of your energy will result in a complete awareness of your true self.

How do you see yourself? Fill in the blanks

Authenticity		Health	
	Balance		Kindness
Concern for others		Service to others	
	Commitment		
	Fairness	Loyalty	Humor

Example

86/4 reflection moves us into the reality of the moment to focus on our deepest values

Concern for others	Excellence	Generosity	Kindness
Compassion	Faith	Geniuses	Openness
Courage	Family	Harmony	Respect for others
Creativity	Friendship	Health	Perseverance
Empathy	Freedom	Service to others	Loyalty
Fairness	Serenity	Honesty	Knowledge
Happiness	Authenticity	Responsibility	Integrity
	Commitment	Balance	

To be or not to be is what you need to answer:

Classical story re-told

Have you ever been fascinated by plays and really paid attention to what is actually being portrayed? To rediscover the answer to the question, let's turn to Shakespeare's classic *Hamlet*.

Note: Not in order on purpose.

Polonius: **"I hear him coming. Let's withdraw, my lord."**

Hamlet: "To be, or not to be? That is the question. Whether 'tis nobler in the mind to suffer the sling and sorrows of outrageous fortune or take arm against a sea of trouble, and, by opposing, end them? To die, to sleep -- no more --and by a sleep to say we end the headache and the thousand natural shocks that flesh is heir to --'tis a consumption devoutly to be wished! To die, to sleep, perchance to dream -- ay, there's the rub, for in sleep of death what dreams may come when we have shuffled off this mortal coil, must give us pause. There's the respect that makes calamity of so long life.'

Polonius: "**I hear him coming. Let's hide, my lord.**"

Hamlet: "The question is: is it better to be alive or dead? Is it nobler to put up with all the nasty things that luck throws your way, or to fight against all those troubles by simply putting an end to them once and for all? Dying, sleeping -- that's all dying is – a sleep that ends all the heartache and shocks that life on earth gives us- that's an achievement to wish for. To die or be in a deep sleep -- to sleep maybe to dream. Ah, but there's the catch: in death sleep who knows what kind of dreams might come, after we've put the noise and commotion of life behind us. This is certainly something to worry about. That's the consideration that makes us stretch out suffering so long.

Polonius: "Ophelia, come here- (to Claudius) your majesty, we will hide. (Ophelia) Appearing natural. Come to think of it, this happens all the time -- people act devoted to God to mask their bad deeds."

Claudius: "Oh, tis too true! How smart a lash that speech doth give my conscience! The harlot's cheek, beautified with plastering art, is not uglier to end the thing that helps it than is my deed to most painted word. O heavy burden!"

Inadequate healthy living will lead to a downward spiral in our overall health, both spiritually, and physically.

Mobilize Yourself

Do not judge by the color of their skin but, by the content of their character. […] I have a dream that one day […] little black boys and black girls will be able to join hands with little white boys and little white girls as sisters and brothers." He painted such concrete images that people knew exactly what they were working toward, even when he was no longer around to offer direction to the movement.

Focus Yourself and Stay <u>Clear Of All</u> <u>Unnecessary Distractions</u>

A big source of stagnation is what we do in our daily lives which serve no true purpose except to distract us. If you want to stay focused on achieving your dreams, you need to eliminate everything in your life that is distracting you.

Some of the common ones are:

- Television
- Video games
- Poor relationships
- Unhealthy food
- Other people's drama

There are many more distractions that you will have to remove from your life. However, the aforementioned have the biggest impact upon your ability to concentrate. Participating in any of them in an excessive manner may cloud your focus and keep you from attaining your goals.

Because some common distractions are addictive, they are difficult to give up. For example, video games and television can be extremely addictive, but giving them up can be a true blessing. No matter how challenging it is, know that it will be worth it in the end.

Keep a Journal

Writing in a journal can be a profound benefit for you. What helps best is writing down your goals and progress. Knowing that you're progressing is a great way to stay motivated. Who wants to keep doing something when they think all their efforts are for nothing? Often our growth and important steps toward our goals are overlooked or ignored. Writing down every single positive step you've taken towards your goals, no matter how small it may seem, will always serve as a reminder that you are progressing, and that reaching your goals happen one step at a time.

Write down some areas in your life that need refinement. Note how you've improved in those areas and what you think you could do to become even better. Here are a few examples:

- Physical
- Mental
- Financial
- Relationships
- Family
- Emotional
- Spiritual

Create New Habits

When you want to move from a habit that you know is holding you back, to one that is beneficial and empowering, the best way to accomplish this is to stick with it for twenty-one days. By doing so, a habit that serves you will form, and you will eventually start doing it with automaticity. After about three to four weeks, you will start noticing the positive changes taking place in your life.

For example, if you want to start going to the gym, mark on a calendar what day and time you want to go. This way, you will always have something to remind you of your goal. After twenty-one days of not giving up, you won't need a calendar anymore, because it will become a habit.

Surround yourself with people that have similar goals

If you're trying to improve your life and remove people who are hindering you from going forward, stop giving your energy to unhealthy, negative relationships and move on. This one can be difficult for a lot of people. Some of us are in relationships, and we have friends that we've known for a long time. Still, they may not support our goals. There's nothing wrong with knowing that you've outgrown someone, especially if they have no desire to improve themselves.

Moving on from people who are holding you back can feel like a weight being lifted off your shoulders. You will notice that when you let go of people that are preventing you from progressing, new ones appear on the scene to help accelerate your goals. It's like being a receiver on a football team. There are defensive players on the opposing team blocking you from catching the ball. However, after a few plays you begin to realize what you need to do to get past the defenders in order to catch the pass for a touchdown.

Take Breaks

Remember there is a big difference between taking some time off and being stagnant. Taking time off recharges and refreshes the mind. For example, nature is calming and creates balance within. Outdoor activities such as hiking or camping impact our well-being. You will always come back with new insights and a focused mind.

Conclusion

Growing and achieving your dreams is meant to be a fun experience. It's what we're here for. It's what we're designed to do. The problem in today's society is that there are so many things that we get caught up in which can have the opposite effect. There are many different obstacles that we must overcome in life, but they don't have to be viewed as negative experiences. Everything you do in life teaches a lesson of some kind, including the most negative experiences, and these experiences often lead to the most important lessons.

It is motivating when you've finally overcome something that is detrimental to your personal growth. Now you are more qualified to help someone who might be going through the same thing. Likewise, once you achieve a goal, you're now in a position to help others who may have that same goal.

Invest in Yourself and <u>Develop Your Skills</u>

Improving your skills doesn't always mean investing in higher education, though that's an option, and perhaps a necessary one depending upon your career field. Investing in your knowledge and skills can take many forms. In addition, expanding your level of knowledge and skill isn't limited to the business arena and doesn't necessarily need to be formal. There are many "skill investment" avenues.

- Advance your education – extra classes, advanced degrees, relevant certifications, are all valuable investments. Take classes, either in person or online.

- Utilize available training – enroll in workshops, attend conferences or participate in webinars.

- Expand your knowledge – there's lots of information available on nearly any subject imaginable. Read books, articles, write papers, anything related to the talent or skill you want to work on. Keep current – stay abreast of the latest trends or advancements. Subscribe to publications, read blogs from experts, and follow the latest news.

Explore your Creative side

There is a fountain of creativity within most of us that has never been tapped or used to its highest potential. We may need to unearth and hone our individual creativity. Creativity, in any form, helps us to grow personally and professionally, to view problems and solutions in different ways, and to utilize other parts of our mind that may have been previously untapped. It's important to keep in mind that creativity has many faces. It's far broader than being a painter or sculptor; it's also about trying new things.

- Learn a new language – take a class or use language training software.

- Try gourmet cooking – enroll in a formal class, by a new cookbook, or ask someone you know who enjoys cooking in a different way.

- Write something – a book, short stories, poetry, anything.

- Explore the outside world – try gardening, bird watching, or landscape photography.

- Enjoy music – play an instrument, learn a new one or join a music group of some kind.

- Create something tangible – paint, sculpt, make pottery, make jewelry or design your own clothes.

Choose some form of activity that you have never tried, haven't practiced in years, or have never explored fully.

Nurture your mind and body

Nurturing both your mind and body allows you to have more to give now and in the future: more energy, more knowledge, more compassion, more ideas, greater strength, and physical and mental endurance.

Expand your mind. Learning new things and keeping your mind active, even in simple ways, helps with growth and maintaining your mental ability.

- Read – anything and everything.

- Explore culture – attend performances, listen to different styles of music, travel, or join an organization or group comprised of people from different backgrounds.

- Open your mind – engage in conversations with those who disagree with you. Look at an argument and try to make a case for the opposing point of view.

- Keep your mind active – play word games, (yes, even Words with Friends counts) or board games that include strategy or try using your brain to perform simple calculations rather than relying on a calculator.

Care for your body. Your body is like a well-oiled machine. If you care for it in the way that you might maintain an expensive car, it will perform marvelously and last for a very long time. Remember the basics:

- Give it high quality fuel – make healthy food choices as often as possible. What you eat determines your energy level and ability to perform. You truly are what you eat.

- Don't push it too hard – rest and relax often, slow down and don't overload your system. Also, don't shift gears too quickly; it causes stress and damage to "your machine," AKA your body.

- Get regular and necessary maintenance – go to the doctor when you're sick; don't wait until you collapse. Better yet, use preventative maintenance -- get check-ups, take appropriate vitamins and pay attention to irregular or erratic symptoms.

- Polish the exterior – take care of the outside too. Many people dismiss this as frivolous and self-indulgent, but it's not, as long as you don't go overboard. I'm not talking about facelifts and Botox; I'm suggesting getting a fabulous haircut and wearing clothes that make you feel confident and attractive.

Investing in yourself truly makes a difference in your life, well-being, and ability to thrive and perform your best. The extent to which you invest in yourself – your mind and your body -- not only shapes the way you interact with the outside world; it often reflects the opinion you have of yourself. Your future is in part determined by your willingness and ability to invest in yourself now.

Channel Yourself -- <u>Clear Your Mind</u>

Breathe in and feel yourself connect to your center, the spirit within you. Breathe out and expand yourself to create more room for the connection to your spirit. Sit or lie down in a comfortable position. Using your diaphragm, inhale quietly through your nose to a count of four. Hold your breath for seven seconds. Exhale completely through your mouth making a whoosh sound. Surrender everything mentally (thoughts), emotionally (feelings) and physically (relax the body) that is not serving your highest purpose in this moment. Continue surrendering and breathing this way through the remainder of the exercise.

Invoke:

Ask Spirit, in whatever Spirit form is special to you, to come into your space to guide and heal you.

Ask:

Write your intention or question down on a pad of paper or journal as you verbalize it out loud.

Receive:

If you were to imagine the answer wafting into your mind, what is it? It might seem like your own thinking, and that is okay, just go with it and write it down as it comes into your mind. Many times, the channeled information begins with a word or phrase, and as you begin writing it unfolds into more detailed answers to your questions. You're essentially having a written and verbal dialogue with Spirit. It may be a few lines to a few pages before you feel the flow. Then your verbiage and writing style may change, using words atypical to your vocabulary.

Apply:

Once you receive your information, the pieces that you resonate with, act on them.

Renew

Practice paying attention to the thoughts going through your mind. The more you do, the easier it will be to notice and to _change your thoughts from what is false and negative to what is true and positive._

Practice paying attention to the messages you listen to. GIGO = Garbage In, Garbage Out. What messages are you exposing your mind, eyes, and ears to? Are the lyrics of the music you listen to consistent with what is "true, good, pure, lovely, and praiseworthy" (see Philippians 4:8)

Have a "go to" truth — such as "God will strengthen me" — or perhaps a Bible verse to help you focus on a better way to renew your mind when you notice you're embracing a lie. For example, when I begin to condemn myself for my failures, I remind myself that God doesn't condemn me (Romans 8:1). Or when I'm tempted to covet, I remind myself that God gives me good things (James 1:17), and if God hasn't given "X" to me, it may not be the right time, or it isn't what is good for me now.

Join a group that can help you in your transformation process. A small group is great for accountability and support.

Pray and ask God to show you what lies you believe, then to show you how to replace them with truth. Ask God to give you a desire for Him and for truth over lies.

 Pause — Slowing down for a moment allows you to hear what's really in your heart so you can make value-driven decisions. Instead of running from one thing to the next, take time to reflect. Stop, take a breath, and ask yourself, "Is this what I really want to do with my life right now? Is there a better — and possibly more fun — way to accomplish this?" Pausing can help you find new approaches to the same old tasks.

Change your mind — Life is a mirror and will reflect back to you what you give out. If you operate on autopilot, you may forget the instructions you've given your subconscious. You may be reinforcing, through your mental habits, the very things you fear. Today, take a few moments to notice and jot down your thoughts. At the end of the day, review any defeatist patterns. If you detect a negative track, replace it with a positive one.

See a new reality— I'm sure you've heard of the statement, "If you can see it, you can be it." For years top athletes have used <u>visualization</u> as a technique to improve their performance. You can use visualization to improve your life by mentally rehearsing your success. If you are unhappy about your current circumstances, then put on your dreaming cap. Imagine your new world. You are the architect of your life and your dreams are the blueprints. Use your imagination and the power of visualization to expand your potential and then take action.

Charge your energy — Pumping up your physical energy can help put you in the right frame of mind for transformation. In addition to releasing mood-enhancing chemicals in the brain, exercise can improve your overall endurance so you can have the staying power to reach your destiny. Your food choices will also make the difference between having clarity or "brain fog."

Release dead weight — Clearing the clutter from your life creates space for the new. As you throw out physical things, you may also need to let go of some people in your current circle. Even though you are the architect of your life, sometimes there is a demolition crew hanging around you waiting to tear things down. Fire them, or at the very least, put them on probation by setting new boundaries.

Shift your surroundings — Stepping away from your current environment can help you change your frame of reference. If you travel for work, take an hour for yourself to simply walk around the locale. If you can't hop on a plane, go to a park you've never visited before. Allow your mind to wander and your senses to take in everything around you. You'll be amazed at how this can spur creativity and spark insights.

Dive into unfamiliar experiences — Doing something you've never done before is a sure way to shake things up. If you usually run, sign up for a tango class instead. If you love food, consider taking a healthy gourmet cooking class. A completely new experience will give you a different perspective, help you make new friends, and allow the brain to make new connections. Remember you don't *have to* do anything. Everything is a choice. Every moment is an opportunity to create the life you want. Whether you're shifting your thoughts or changing your environment, the power is in your hands.

Expand

The reason the questions below are so important is because the answers will lead to self-actualization -- the realization of one's potentiality and talents. Once you discover those things, you no longer live unconsciously from moment to moment, or just go through the motions. Self-actualization awakens the deeper significance of your choices, the energy you are broadcasting to the world, what you are inviting into your life, and what you are making others aware of.

This is your life; it is your signature creation. It is your duty to live true to yourself, with integrity and authenticity communicating your message to the world.

Your life's mission is not to make a few million dollars, although that may be an achievable goal. What I'm going to say next may be controversial. Your life's mission is to love yourself, to learn to love what you have, and to create what you love and love what you create.

Your life is about expanding your awareness, expanding your vision of yourself and your life, until it is the greatest possible version of who you are and who you wish to be in your incarnated human form. Without loving yourself, how can you hope to achieve much? Nothing will ever truly satisfy you. And then you will live a life of perpetually seeking, searching, yearning...

Without giving love to yourself first, how will you be able to give to others? Feeding and nourishing yourself will automatically feed and nourish others if you set this as your intention. Teach a man to love himself, and he will forever be able to love others. This creates unimaginable possibilities, as it allows creation from a sound foundation.

Questions to ask.

- Do you love yourself enough to forgive yourself?
- Do you love yourself enough to forgive others?
- Do you love yourself enough to nourish your body with life-affirming nutrient-rich food, the way nature intended, or do you feed yourself processed non-foods, sugar-foods, etc.?
- Do you love yourself enough to exercise your body, stretch it, build your physical resilience and strength, and continually improve your body's conditioning?
- Do you love yourself enough to feed your soul with whatever your heart intends?
- Do you love yourself enough to live in the moment, to forget the past, not worry about the future, but to be truly present to the opportunity within every moment?
- Do you love yourself enough to commit to your decisions, to take action that serves your spirit with all your heart? Do you believe that if you want to go somewhere, you'll only get halfway with half your heart in it?
- Do you love yourself enough to consistently expand your mind, by learning new things, and continually grow your expertise about

life? With more knowledge about life, you'll have greater awareness and ability to deal with any event.

- Do you love yourself enough to have fun, allow your soul to be joyful, do the things you love doing, release stress, relax your mind, body and soul, and take the time to rejuvenate and re-energize?
- Do you love yourself enough to rest sufficiently – to sleep enough?

Now, more than ever, we need to ask ourselves who we want to be in an age of possibility. We need to examine our foundations, the very fabric of our being, and our position in the world. As the world presents a mirror to the internal landscape, examining what is happening within, will always guide and clarify external events.

Look within for your answers. If you build stable, healthy, well-balanced self-love, self-respect and self-appreciation, your foundation is in place to build the same things in your external world. Loving yourself is the foundation for living a fully self-actualized life. With love, the world was created, and with love it continues to thrive. Expanding that energy within you expands the energy of life and expands the DNA of success. Go with an open heart, go with a full heart, and go soundly into the world with love.

"Wherever you go, go with all your heart."
Confucius

To transform mind, body and spirit requires cultivating self-love.

Here are SIX KEYS that transformed my life:

<u>Activate awareness of self and self-talk</u>. What do you say to yourself perpetually? Do you listen to your thoughts, filter them, and question them?

<u>Clean and purify the body vessel</u>. Your body is your temple. It serves you. It represents you. If you do not treat it as such, you're unlikely to develop or enhance self-love. Destroying your body does the opposite of engendering self-love; it is self-defeating. Your body not only serves you, it is also your manifesto. Treat it as sacred.

<u>Spiritual Refinement</u>. When you connect to the essence of spirit, something changes within. It doesn't matter what your spiritual or religious beliefs are, even if you believe in nothing, or you're an atheist. What matters is that you practice refinement of the soul. If you don't already have a daily devotion like prayer or meditation, explore the available options or create your own daily practice. It is never too late to start. For some, it is time spent playing or listening to music that uplifts their soul. For others, it is a combination of things. I have never heard anyone declare that their spirituality is connected to watching television, being stuck in traffic or working a 9 to 5 job. Make the time to develop a relationship with yourself by doing something that uplifts you.

Personal Communion. Every day, you require "me" time in order to be centered. This is not selfish; instead, it is essential for personal well-being. In this time, you can develop your thinking and refine your sensibilities. It may be in the form of a quiet nature walk, a relaxing bath, or time alone in meditation. Your greatest investment is YOU!

Develop a Personal Vision and Purpose. What are you doing here? Just waiting for the weekend to start, or for the next TV show to begin? Or is there something deeper, greater, bigger, and bolder? Is there some goal that is beyond yourself, something that defines who you want to be, your statement to the world? Develop a personal mission statement that works according to your values. This is the next step in your personal evolution and happiness -- stating who you are to the world.

Your life is your practice. Ultimately, your lifetime is a sum of actions, experiences and how you spent your time. How would you wish to be remembered?

Your life is your practice – so how would you wish to spend it? Only you can answer this question.

Create an exercise using the 6 processes

Work it out (Intro Exercise)

- What do I believe?

```



```

- What are my values?

```



```

- Is what I believe in line with my life?

```



```

- Where are you going and how do you plan on getting there?

```



```

- Who do you deeply respect?

```
_____
_____
_____
_____
```

- When are you at your best?

```
_____
_____
_____
_____
```

- What are your goals for work/career vision that reflect your personal vision and values?

```
_____
_____
_____
_____
```

- How are you contributing to the well-being of those around you?

```
_____
_____
_____
_____
```

- Think of someone you respect and name three things you admire about them.

```
_____
_____
_____
_____
```

- What is the one inscription that captures who you really are and inspire to be in life?

What We Do Daily Causes Success or Failure

Transformation of one's life begins with conception. Can we agree that conception is the capacity, function or process of forming or understanding ideas or abstractions? Biologically, conception is the moment when the sperm cell from a male breach the ovum of a female. So, let's resolve that our transformation is when we are pregnant with the idea of becoming.

Conception can be viewed as the forming or devising of a plan or idea, the timing between a product's conception and its launch.

Unit 1: Transformation is Choice

When we begin this paradigm shift in our thinking, we must be mentally & physically prepared. The same is true for all our interactions.

All behaviors are purposeful. We attempt, given our current knowledge and skills, to meet one or more of the basic human needs -- that is, needs which evolved over time and have become part of our genetic structure. These needs are the general motivations for everything we do.

Our basic needs are:

- Survival – this choice is a physiological need. This includes the need for food, shelter and safety, because we have genetic instruction to survive.
- Love and belonging -- the need to love and a longing for relationship and social connections, to give and receive affection and feel part of a group.
- Power –this is to be competent. To be skilled, to be recognized for our achievements and skills to be listened to and have a sense of self-worth.
- Freedom – the need for independence, autonomy, to have a choice and to be able to take control of the direction of one's life.
- Happiness/Fun – the need for happiness and to find pleasure, should you doubt that this is important as any other need, just imagine a life without hope of any enjoyment. All of the inhabitants of the universe enjoy having fun.

The characteristics of the above are:

- Universal
- Innate
- Overlapping
- Moment to moment
- Conflict/Others Needs

You always have a destination or a goal to reach. The process of attaining those goals includes choices. Within those choices you determine how you will communicate with others. Will you seek assistance from others, or will you achieve the task alone? Our goal is to lead you toward a decision that reflects beliefs and skill sets that will help you change the direction of your life, the essence of your home, and the vitality of your community.

What are Your Core Beliefs?

What is the center of who you are, and what makes you do what you do? For instance, do you believe in anything? Do you believe that all people want, need and deserve to be whole and treated the way you want to be treated? Do you treat people the way you want to be treated?

Key Principles

What we see in ourselves is what is reflected around us, based on our own understanding of self. We all have needs to feel valued, respected, to give and receive support, and to be heard. We must acknowledge meeting these needs and prevailing over obstacles. We have to embrace the core value of uniting as one.

Situational Awareness Guide

Situational awareness is the ability to identify, process, and comprehend the critical elements of information. More simply put, it knows what is going on around you. Traffic signs guide us safely to our destination. What are your traffic signals? Are you being led safely to your destination?

Your Basic Beliefs

How much of your belief system do you really believe? What if nothing really mattered? What if people didn't respect each other nor believe in meeting the needs of others? Success would not exist if we lived in this state of mind. People would not believe in anything. Without a belief system, there would be no morality.

We all can improve, but do we want to?

How do we get there?

- Respect one another.
- Unite as one – we are stronger when our skills and operate as a unit.
- Value our differences – it takes every member to operate in one direction.

43

- Support others.
- Build trust – each member must recognize each other's talents and build up, not tear down, those talents.
- You determine who you are.

Unit 2: Transformation is a Personal Shift

Effectiveness is a shifting away of all you think you are and becoming totally engrossed with the needs of another.

- Dignity and respect.
- To listen and understand.
- To be involved in a meaningful way.
- To build trust and value.
- To be supported.
- To encourage.
- To strengthen relationships because we believe in them.
- To help meet goals.

The practical approach:

- Share with one another.
- Resolve our differences to see the common thread that binds us.

- Commitment – does not come without distraction.
- Govern our approach – we do not pay attention to how we move in conversation, but we speak before we listen.
- Encourage – always build up.

Life is about choices and with those choices come struggle. When we approach life with esteem, empathy, involvement, and support, we enact the principles of unselfishness. Unselfishness embraces the fundamental practices of love and understanding. It does not demand its own way. It's not irritable towards others, nor rude or boastful. It doesn't keep record of wrongdoing, nor is it jealous. It does not rejoice in injustice but rejoices whenever truth wins. It never gives up and never loses faith. Unselfishness is always hopeful and endures through every circumstance.

Embracing others is the key to effectively enhancing the self-esteem of others. It is to be both specific and sincere in its nature.

Unit 3: Transformation is a Personal Shift in Action

Every action, every thought, every moment, is either creating the life you desire or tearing down the foundation of your desires.

Often people have grand desires, but their actions don't reflect those hopes. On the contrary, their actions, thoughts, words, and deeds destroy their hopes and desires at the very root.

Instead of dedicating their life to *"build"* upon their desires, they "hide out," hoping their wishes will somehow come to pass. All the while, they do nothing daily to guarantee the manifestation of those things that they supposedly crave most.

The desired outcome is predicated upon what comes from inside you. It is not a force that can be manipulated. Although you will experience both, whatever you feed the most will govern you.

Happiness is not something that comes to you. It is something that is created in you by experience. It gives you faith for today and hope for tomorrow. Your faith is tied to your happiness. However, they do not exist in the absence of peace. It's your attitude. When we adopt a positive attitude, life becomes rewarding and adventurous, instead of something to get through. Each day should bring newfound experiences that are reflective of what's in our hearts, and this could be negative or positive.

Unit 4: Transformation is a Personal Shift to Gratitude

Thankfulness:

It is the place where the development of awareness resides with humility. It recognizes that an attitude of gratitude in everything produces happiness. Despite what appears as a setback, it's a step forward toward achieving something bigger and better than your current situation. It's not looking at what is, but rather what can be. It will unlock inner keys to achieve:

- Fullness of life.
- What we have into enough and more.
- Denial into acceptance.
- Chaos into order.
- Confusion into clarity.
- A meal into a feast.
- A house into a home.
- Stranger into a friend.

It will make the past clear and bring peace into today, which produces a vision for tomorrow

Unit 5: Transformation is a Personal Shift in Awareness

Pay Attention. Pay Attention. Pay Attention.

What captures your attention?

		MUSIC
TV		

How are you spending your time? Do you find yourself running from work to school to activities, then back home, only to start the next 86/4 the same way?

Most people don't pay attention to what they say or to what they do. Let's shift our gears and focus on communication.

What governs our conversation?

Could it be that our actions play an important part in what comes out of us? Can we agree that what we think is governed by what we ingest? The input penetrates our thoughts, which enters our heart and causes our mouth to speak. If what comes out your mouth is a stream of negativity, you will become hopeless and blind yourself to the light in front of you. Do we, or can we, deliberately pay attention to everything we say? When you catch yourself saying something negative, ask yourself this question, "Is this I really want?" We reap what we sow. The power of life and death is in the tongue. To many, this may be far from the reality of what is happening in society. Hence, I have introduced quantum physics in our pattern of reasoning.

Scientific Example

There is an area of research in science called quantum physics. Quantum physicists will tell you atoms, neutrons and protons actually respond to human words. Scientists have literally watched atoms, neutrons and protons become excited and respond positively as positive words were spoken to them. They also watched atoms; neutrons and protons slow down, become irresponsive and seemingly lifeless as negative words were spoken to them.

Can we comprehend what we just read? It is the source of everything in existence that lives -- atoms, neutrons and protons -- respond negatively or positively depending on the words being spoken over them. This is a scientific fact. The core source of spirituality understood the law of quantum physics way back before anything was ever created (Colossians 1:16). Yet, there is something even

49

more fascinating about quantum physics. The same scientists have discovered that by simply looking at those same neutrons and protons moving within an atom, they can also have an effect upon them. When they **expected** the neutrons and protons to stop moving as a result of being looked at, they did. When they **did not expect** the neutrons and protons to stop moving within the atom, they did not.

You may fundamentally disagree, but this certainly confirms foundational core principles of spirituality and scriptural teaching in regard to the power of words and how they affect our lives by <u>speaking</u> and <u>expecting our words to come to pass.</u> Expectation really is the key to life.

This, of course, has made believers out of many quantum physicists. However, some physicists who have witnessed this phenomenon were not convinced because it contradicted their studies regarding the origin of life. Therefore, these scientists insist there has been no such discovery.

Unit 6: Transformation is a Personal Shift in belief

There's a Miracle in Your Mouth

It's Just Simple Quantum Physics, That's All

"He answered and said unto them, Verily I say unto you, If ye have faith, and doubt not, ye shall not only do this which is done to the fig tree, but also if ye shall say unto this mountain, Be thou removed, and be thou cast into the sea; it shall be done. And all things, whatsoever ye shall ask in prayer, believing, ye shall receive." (Matthew 21:21, 22).

Many of us have been around the Word of Faith long enough to know that He said we can have what we say. Of course, we can only have what we say when it is based upon what He has already agreed to do in the Word. The definition of His teaching reflects in us understanding of scriptural promises that line up with His words that we believe, which ultimately come forth out of our heart, which cause us to speak them.

Example

In Matthew 21:21, it says, "I tell you the truth, if you have faith and don't doubt, you can do things like this and much more. You can even say to this mountain, 'May you be lifted up and thrown into the sea,' and it will happen."

The reference is referring to mountains of human obstacles or problems.

"…Not by might, nor by power, but by My Spirit [of whom the oil is a symbol], says the Lord of hosts. For who are you, O GREAT MOUNTAIN [OF HUMAN OBSTACLES]?" (Zechariah 4:6, 7 Amplified Bible)

It is pretty obvious here that God, like Zechariah, was making reference to human obstacles when He referred to the mountain in Matthew 21:21. We can take the Word and stand up to any obstacle that confronts us, commanding the obstacle to be removed and it must obey.

What is your obstacle?

- Sickness by the very word of your mouth
- Financial
- Emotional
- Moral

- Social

Have you agreed to do something about your obstacle? Have you begun to speak a promise (or solution) over the obstacle (or the problem)?

If the answer is no, it's because you have not used your faith to speak life over your problems. I believe these keys will help you receive the promise.

- Turn away from all negative communication. If you don't refrain from negative communication, you validate what you are feeling. Therefore, you'll continue down the same road. The pendulum continues in doubt, sickness, failure, rejection, and destruction.
- Recognize your need for help.

"For every kind of beasts, and of birds, and of serpents, and of things in the sea, is tamed, and hath been tamed of mankind: BUT THE TONGUE CAN NO MAN TAME; it is an unruly evil, full of deadly poison. Therewith bless us God, even the Father; and therewith curse we men, which are made after the similitude of God. Out of the same mouth proceeds blessings and cursing's. My brethren, these things ought not so to be." (James 3:7-10).

"If any of you lacks wisdom, let him ask of Him/God, that giveth to all men liberally, and upbraided not; and it shall be given him." (James 1:5).

James said God would give liberally all of the supernatural help needed to tame that wild tongue of yours before you kill yourself or someone else with it. (See Matthew 12:35-37, Mark 11:23, Psalm 141:3, Proverbs 18:21.)

Pay attention! Pay Attention! Decide to teach yourself.

Many years after Thomas Edison's mother died, he became one of the greatest inventors the world had ever known. One day, he was looking through old family keepsakes. He came upon a folded piece of paper, which had been left in the corner of a desk drawer. It was the note he had carried home from school as a little boy for his mother to read.

He opened it and read, "Your son is addled (mentally ill). We won't let him come to school anymore."

Thomas Edison cried for hours that day before writing in his diary, "Thomas Alva Edison was an addled child that, by a hero mother, became the genius of the century."

Thomas' mother, Nancy, would not believe the words of failure written and spoken over her child by his teacher. Nor would she repeat them or even allow him to hear them.

As a result, her son grew to be a man who exerted a degree of power in the world of technology of which no one ever dreamed for him - no one but his mother.

Although his mother died when he was only twenty-four years old, Thomas said of her, "My mother was the making of me. She was so true, so sure of me. I felt I had something to live for, someone I must not disappoint."

If you do not have that positive force of reinforcement from someone else, let those words come from your own mouth.

As was the case with Nancy Edison and her little boy, Thomas, anyone can remove obstacles with faith-filled words.

Despite our circumstances, we simply must speak positive words daily within the 86/4 that we are given. This is when our circumstances will come in line with what He desires for us.

"Death and life are in the power of the tongue, and they that love it shall eat the fruit thereof." (Proverbs 18:21).

- People who speak words of death eat the fruit of death.

- People who speak words of life eat the fruit of life.

- It's not up to anyone else how successful we are. It's up to us and the words we speak over our lives.

Someone said, "Well, I don't believe in all that positive confession stuff. It doesn't work. No matter how hard I try, it just doesn't work for me." I told that person, "Sure, it does. It's working for you now. You keep saying it does not work no matter how hard you try. Therefore, the harder you try, the more it does not work. You've got the thing in reverse with the accelerator to the floor. Why don't you put that power to work for you instead of against you?"

"Beat your plowshares into swords and your pruning hooks into spears":

"LET THE WEAK SAY, I AM STRONG." (Joel 3:10)

"Take your words, and turn to the Lord: say unto him, take away all iniquity, and receive us graciously: SO, WILL WE RENDER THE CALVES OF OUR LIPS." (Hosea 14:2).

The Hebrew word for "calves" in this verse is actually "sacrifice."

- It takes faith and sacrifice to say, "You are just going to have to endure."

Keep speaking faith words. Things are happening behind the scenes. The same principles that were once your problems are now your solutions.

"A good man out of the good treasure of the heart brings forth good things: and an evil man out of the evil treasure brings forth evil things. But I say unto you, that every idle word that men shall speak, they shall give account thereof in the Day of Judgment. FOR BY THY WORDS THOU SHALT BE JUSTIFIED, AND BY THY WORDS THOU SHALT BE CONDEMNED." (Matthew 12:35-37)

"THROUGH FAITH WE UNDERSTAND THAT THE WORLDS WERE FRAMED BY THE WORD OF FAITH, so that things which are seen were not made of things which do appear." (Hebrews 11:3)

"Who being the brightness of his glory, and the express image of his person, and UPHOLDING ALL THINGS BY THE WORD OF HIS POWER, when he had by himself purged our sins, sat down on the right hand of the Majesty on high." (Hebrews 1:3)

Have you ever thought that your present position in life could be reflective of the words spoken over you? These could be directly spoken or believing what someone else has said about you. If your present situation is not reflective of what you want, you are frustrated with your present condition. Begin to move in the right direction by transforming your thoughts and conversation to reveal what you believe by speaking positive words. You can position yourself by becoming the catalyst for allowing what is right and spiritually correct into your belief system.

"Behold also the ships, which though they be so great, and are driven by fierce winds, yet are they turned about with a very small helm, whithersoever the governor desire. Even so the tongue is a little member and boasted great things. Behold how great a matter a little fire kinglet! And THE TONGUE IS A FIRE, A WORLD OF INIQUITY: so is the tongue among our members, that it defiles the whole body, and sets on fire the course of nature, and it is set on fire of hell" (James 3:4-6).

Are you destroying yourself and your loved ones by letting your tongue do its own thing independent of your brain and spirit? Or, are you blessing your loved ones with your words?

Thomas Alva Edison was an American inventor, scientist, and businessman from Milan, Ohio who literally changed the world with his inventions. He lived from 1847 to 1931. At the time of his death, he had accumulated 2,332 patents worldwide for his inventions.

Among Edison's inventions were the incandescent light bulb, the phonograph cylinder for recording music and voices, the phonograph machine, the carbon microphone, the movie camera, electric power distribution for city and statewide usage, the electrographic vote counter, the electric generator, the alkaline battery, the mimeograph (copy) machine and the world's first cement mixing machine.

It is said of Thomas A. Edison, "He invented the future."

One day as a boy Thomas Edison came home from school and gave a note to his mother. He told her, "My teacher gave this paper to me and told me to only give it to my mother."

Thomas' mother's eyes were tearful as she ignored the words the teacher had written and instead spoke these words aloud to him: "Your son is a genius. This school is too small for him and doesn't have enough good teachers to train him. **Please teach him yourself**."

It's time to stop using your mouth to mess up your world. It's time to start using your mouth to create the kind of world you want to live in.

Unit 7: Transformation is a Personal Shift in Attitude

Get inspired

Succeeding and changing requires a strong intention to succeed. It is not secondary to anything; it must be first. If you really want something, you'll invent amazing ways to achieve it.

Get passion

When you are inspired, it invokes passion. Having the passion outside of who we are and putting our focus toward success involves empowering others with passion.

Get Attitude!

Attitude Is Infectious

Your attitude is the first thing people pick up during face-to-face communication. Just as laughing, yawning, and crying are infectious, attitude is infectious. Before you say a word, your attitude can affect the people you meet and influence their behavior. Somehow just by looking or feeling; you can be infected by another person's attitude and *vice versa*. When you are operating from a useful attitude-- such as enthusiasm, curiosity, and humility -- your body language tends to take care of it and sends out signals of openness.

Attitude Drives Behavior

Attitudes drive behavior. If you want to **succeed** at anything you need to have the **right mindset**. Your body language is a result of your mental attitude. By choosing your attitude, you get into that mood and send out a message that everyone understands, **consciously or unconsciously**.

Almost always, you have a choice as to what attitude to adopt. There is nothing in any normal work situation that dictates you must act one way or the other. If you feel angry about something that happens, for instance, that's how you choose to feel. The event does not have the power in to make you feel that way. It's what you give your energy to. It is your choice. And since you do have a choice, most of the time you'll be better off if you choose to react in a positive, rather than a negative, way.

- We are what we **think**.
- Wherever you go, **go with all your heart**.
- There is time to be **courageous**, and there is time to **be afraid**.
- The spiritual effectiveness of all endeavors depends on the **inner attitude**.
- Whatever you do, always do it honestly (Do not cheat yourself).
- The future belongs to the common man with uncommon determination.

Power has been given to all men and women. Only those who dare to humble themselves will experience the true essence of who they are by serving others!

Beauty is an Attitude

Due to the narrow **definition** of **beauty**, we are left with the task of redefining **beauty**. I strongly agree that **beauty** can be achieved through **attitude**, spirit, and faith. Faith in a loving and forgiving God will be the root of any and **all** manifestations of **beauty**. One of life's beauties is solidified in a loving heart and a heart of a laboring hand. You can have all the exterior beauty, but without depth of a kind soul it is merely decoration. Inward beauty revives our soul. It ignites the passion we thought was gone and unlocks the potential behind every situation. It opens closed doors, restores dreams, and brings light into the darkness. Believing the best is yet to come enables us to walk in dignity through every circumstance we face. It gives us strength to fight, courage to listen, and the ability to conquer giants and become the person God created us to be.

What would your life look like if you refused to doubt? What would our world look like if we put action behind our words and truly believed?

- Your attitude
- Your Spirit
- Your Faith
- Your Heart
- Your Dignity

Nothing can stop the man with the right mental attitude from achieving his goal; nothing on earth can help the man with the wrong mental attitude.
                                        ~ Thomas Jefferson

There is little difference in people, but that little difference makes a big difference. This little difference is attitude. The big difference is whether it is positive or negative.

~ Clement W. Stone

Our lives begin to end the day we become silent about things that matter.

~ Martin Luther King, Jr.

The activist is not the man who says the river is dirty. The activist is the man who cleans up the river.

~ Ross H. Perot

Thomas Alva Edison's Mother Spoke Words of Faith

For true success, ask yourself these four questions:

- Why?
- Why not?
- Why not me?
- Why not now?

UNIT 8: Transformation Revealed

It's no secret that people with positive attitudes thrive, while those with negative ones can wither. But how do you build a positive lifestyle? And once you build it, how do you maintain it? What you have learned will help you ascertain where you are, assist you in understanding why you're there, and then show you how to build and energize your inner self and engage your mind, spirit, and your body.

HOW DOES CHANGE HAPPEN? ACTION STARTS WITH ALIGNMENT.

Build your positive self now! How does change happen?

To stack the deck of cards in your favor, build on your strengths to reach the degree of excellence you're trying to reach. It's important to first look at why you changed what happened and what elements — big and small — impacted you:

Shifting Dynamics

When the core of all you are becoming has emerged, it often leads to uncertainty.

Positive people see this as an opportunity to continue developing. They are willing to invest in evaluating and improving processes and strategies to enhance what is taking place inside.

Leadership Changes

Without a transition plan in place you often fail to move forward or lose ground, which can be detrimental to the intended goal. The key to the longevity of anyone experiencing changes is to move in the intended direction in spirit, in soul and in body, with the same vision and strategy, focused on internal and external development.

Structure

Transformation and development changes can lead to changes in external relationships, which in turn can lead to a lack of communication internally and externally. These changes can directly impact how you view your developmental outcomes.

Growth

Your growth process is and will forever be changing. Moving may require taking one step at a time. The important thing is to continue in a state of motion, as this leads to your development. Consistency throughout the growth process is key to maintaining a positive outcome where excellence is a priority.

Action Starts with Alignment

A positive mindset always starts with your intention. Your mind and heart must be aligned with the objective you want to create — and it must understand the desire in creating it.

How do you know if you're leaning positive or negative?

Your organizational culture leans positive if it has:

- Motivation.
- Strong leadership.
- Clear and open direction.
- Focus on excellence.
- Strong internal and external relationships.
- Opportunity for upward growth

If your organization shows these qualities, it points to a negative culture:

- Difficult communication.
- Preoccupation with external issues.
- Unhealthy internal relationships.
- Acceptance of doing only the bare minimum.

Get It Done

There's always room for improvement and growth. The truth is that it's never finished. Even if you have developed a positive outlook, there's always room for improvement and growth.

Accountability

When you start to demonstrate a positive attitude daily, open and clear communication brings it all together. Through established behaviors, standards, training, and feedback, you will see a better you. By establishing standards, behaviors, measurement and accountability, you can then reward and recognize accomplishment.

Attitude Measurement Behaviors

Your behavior must match the vision and values of your objective. The systems and procedures you have in place must work for your intended goal.

Vision and Values

Your vision and values are at the heart of your development. Everything you do starts with this. Standards of living are the keys to consistency

- Communication establishes accountability systems that link to your spirit, soul, and body.
- Build your positive self without losing your mind.

Being a change agent for yourself is never easy. In fact, many efforts fail outright. Many others never achieve their original visions. This workbook is designed to help you think about change in a way that will involve the people who can best help you become successful.

The truth is that every one of us undergoes change. Some of the most common drivers these days include: Changing friendships/relationships, marriages, job changes, and changes brought on by having children. So, change is ubiquitous.

Why Change Fail

These are the most cited reasons for failure in transition:

• Resistance to change

• No consensus

• No champion

• Unrealistic expectations

A close look at that list reveals an important insight. Change usually fails when you fail to manage yourself in the equation. Getting that right involves putting critical elements in place, which we will explore next.

Misguided and poorly planned change efforts often follow winding and confusing roads. Before we start, consider this question: How is success defined and measured?

Here's a hint: Success cannot be measured by results alone.

To achieve true, balanced success, you must look beyond results to how the results are achieved (process), and to relationships.

This model is useful in determining goals and the measures of success in any endeavor.

Often, the "process" and "relationship" dimensions are leading indicators of what you can expect in terms of "results." Balancing results, process and relationship creates sustainable change, with greater satisfaction.

The question, "What's your current state?" is a description of what currently exists in your life. The future state is a clear picture of what will exist in the future when the change is complete.

The pathway to action – At a strategic level, this launches and articulates the project plan, and describes the streams of work necessary to ensure the future state is accomplished.

Assess contextual factors that will affect the planning process, including important changes in the external environment since the last planning process.

Context
- Where are we?
- Where do we want to go?
- How do we get there?

Where Are We? Assess the current reality, including:
- Strengths
- Opportunities for improvement
- Relationships

Where are we going? Build an initial agreement around future directions, including:

- Hopes and visions of success in the future values that will support, inform, and guide the objective.

How will we get there? Designing the pathway to action

Design and implement a planning process (Pathway to action) that will result in an action plan that guides objectives. The action plan must include, among other elements:

- Specific goals and objectives.
- Relationship involvement.
- Implementation strategies and plans.
- Plans for monitoring success and ensuring sustainability.

You can't just build it. You've got to sustain it. One of the most critical things you can do early on is identify someone to hold you accountable.

The case for change

The most difficult case for change and building support is one of the most practical tools we offer. One critical job of a change is to communicate only the benefits and potential for change.

Why a case for change is important?

1. To build commitment.

2. To clarify why.

3. To uncover expectations and hopes.

4. To outline goals and milestones.

Create and communicate a vision

While a mission, a strategy, and goals provide direction for actions and decisions, a vision provides inspiration. People need inspiration in times of change. Vision is a picture of the future that is clear enough to show people what life could be like if they succeed. It is set in the future, far enough out to allow time for real change to occur, but not so distant that's too abstract or lofty. A vision describes what will be in place, not the action plan on how to get there.

Proverbs 23:7

For as he thinketh in his heart, so is he.

The importance of a man's thoughts

1. A man is as his thoughts.

2. A man has control over his thoughts.

3. God helps him in the exercise of that control.

"We are that really, both to God and to man, which we are inwardly." (*Matthew Henry.*)

Thoughts

I. The infinite importance of men's thoughts. This text, in counselling for a particular case, and bidding us test the sincerity of one who invites us, asserts a principle of wide application. You do not know a man until you know his thoughts. God knows him perfectly, because He knows his thoughts.

1. You cannot know a man merely by listening to his words or watching his actions. There is always more, and often better, in men than comes into expression.

2. The revelations of close and trustful friendships are revelations of the thoughts.

3. The claims of God reach beyond right action, and demand right thought. The law of God searches the secret intents of the heart.

4. The redemption that is provided includes in its scheme the sanctification of the very thought.

5. All sin is represented as springing up out of, and finding expression for, lust in the sphere of thought. The unrestrained of thought often comes to us in the form of feeling and the mastery of sin.

II. The amount of control man has over his thoughts. If he had no control over them his moral responsibility would be gone. We cannot help the evil thoughts coming to us. We have control--

1. The material of our thoughts. The materials are the sum of past impressions. Thinking is the combining, comparing, and rearranging of the actual contents of the mind. We can direct ourselves away from the evil and towards the good. We can fill our minds with good suggestions and associations. Illustrate from going into scenes suggestive of vice; reading questionable or immoral books, etc.

2. The processes of thought. There may be the nourishing of the evil. There may be the swaying of the mind through the power of the renewed will, and with the help of the indwelling Spirit. Apply to wandering thoughts in the house of God. Do we make the mastery of such evil the subject of real effort?

The thoughts of the heart the best evidence of a man's spiritual state

The knowledge of ourselves is one of the most noble and excellent attainments in human life. He that knows himself stands fair for immortal felicity. The thoughts of men's hearts do evidence what their spiritual state is. These do ordinarily give the best and surest measure of the frame of men's minds. What thoughts, then, evidence the spiritual state of men? Not occasional thoughts. Not such as arise from strong convictions that come on us suddenly. Not such as arise from apparent Divine desertions. Despairing thoughts are no sure evidence of the condition of souls. Not such as arise from violent temptations. Not such as arise from men's calling and manner of life. Not such as arise from attendance upon, and the performance of, religious duties. The religious discourse of others may produce pious thoughts in an unregenerate person. A man may read God's Word and be yet far from the kingdom. So, he may attend the preaching of the Word, and even pray, without having more than surface thoughts. Answering the question affirmatively, mention may be made of voluntary thoughts, such as the mind is apt for and inclines towards. Let us each see to it that our thoughts be such as evidence us to be holy persons. Practice frequent, serious, and close examination.

Situational awareness

This is the most important skillset when it comes to your well-being. By practicing situational awareness, you can avoid being in dangerous situations, possibly involving another person, unsafe driving conditions or any number of other things.

I define situational awareness as the ability to take in information about those around you, your surroundings as well self-analysis, interpret that information and act accordingly to your current situation. To fully develop this, I'll briefly explore the tree aspects of situational awareness.

Awareness around You

Coopers Color Code is absolutely a part of situational awareness. To be fully aware of any given situation you need to be aware of more than just whether someone an immediate threat to you. For instance, let's say you are in a room with twelve other people. You are in Condition Yellow of Coopers Color Code and have assessed that no one is an immediate threat to your safety. If you take in the entire situation, you might notice that the gentleman a few seats away on your left is sweating and rubbing his left arm. You might also notice that the couple to your right is having an argument, albeit a quiet argument, but an argument, nonetheless.

You can learn a lot from just watching people. They often tell you things they wouldn't say with their mouths. In fact, I think more people tell the truth with their actions than they do with their lips. This by itself isn't enough to be fully aware; it is just one piece of the puzzle.

Awareness in your Surroundings

Being aware of your surroundings means not only paying attention to what you see but often what you don't, comparing what is normal to what you have in front of you and assessing it and looking for things that are irregular.

Here is an example of something standing out from what you are used to seeing. You often stop at Starbucks for coffee at 6:00 am. There are a few cars in the parking lot; lights on inside and you can see the employees working. If, one morning, you pull up and there are cars in the lot but there are no lights on and no one answers the drive-thru, the differences should be setting off some alarm bells.

Here is an example of something you might not see often but that you have to assess, depending on what you believe to be normal; you are finishing up your Christmas shopping at a popular mall and notice a backpack that is sitting on the floor, partially hidden, with no one near it. This is abnormal as you would normally expect to see people near the bag.

Awareness of Self

We're all aware of what mood we're in or how we feel about something, but sometimes we might not know why. For instance, there have been times when I've met someone and almost instantly wanted to do something. Does it make sense? No, not really. Should I feel that way? No, probably not. Should I pay attention to it? Absolutely, yes! I'm not easily angered, so when someone does anger me, I immediately go to Condition Orange and pay close attention to them.

There are often things that our subconscious picks up on that we often don't "see" right away, if at all. Call it intuition, your gut or the Holy Spirit, but when something inside starts sounding alarms do not silence them with logic. I think women have an easier time with this. Men can feel shame when feelings of fear, anger or other "bad" emotions come to the surface, so we ignore or explain them away.

Sometimes awareness of one of these is enough to get you to take action, sometimes it could take more. The more you practice situational awareness, the easier it will become to notice things that would normally have gone unnoticed. If you think you could use some help increasing your situational awareness, I will share some tips with you.

Awareness is a choice. One has to choose to pay attention. But once that choice is made, the part of the brain responsible for monitoring the senses, known as the Reticular Activating System (RAS) takes over. It switches filters on and off that will fulfill your subconscious desire to pay attention. By simply telling yourself to pay attention to certain things, the RAS will scan for and acknowledge those things when it encounters them.

The Truth in us Manifested

I hope you find inspiration here, as you discover the depth and fullness of your power and potential.

My goal is to help your mind open to know
the power of the love within you. No matter where
we are on this life journey, we never come to the
limit of love's power in our lives. The more we
use love, the more powerful it becomes in us. There

is always opportunity to take one more step. Seeing life through the lens of love opens greater truth and meaning in all experiences.

While we can't change experiences of the past, we can increase our understanding, resolutions, and growth that come from challenging experiences. Challenges are opportunities to renew motivation and to transcend limiting perceptions. As we grow, we create more of love's power and life's full potential.

Perceptions create patterns of behavior. Loving perceptions bring power into our choices and actions. This powerful and active love creates the fullness and meaning for a joyful life.

I am honored to offer support and guidance as we journey together in this unique and precious life.

Let the words of my mouth be seasoned by His word

The primary purpose of communication is to express you. As you express yourself, you build relationships. You can only be loved in a relationship to the degree you are known. Love and wisdom create powerful communication. This powerful communication creates lasting joy in your life and the lives of others. Express yourself!

What does it mean to express myself from a place of love and wisdom? When I nourish my mind with empathy and compassion, my heart can use communication to create connection.

Love and wisdom must create the intention for the message. Attention to one's intent is critical to establishing healthy connections.

Know your goal for the communication. Without love and wisdom in the goal, the content in the message lacks power. The goal must be within your ability to accomplish.

Toxic emotions poison messages meant to share love and wisdom. If your communication will contain toxic emotions, change yourself. Be clear with yourself about the intent of your communication. Destructive communication occurs when a person uses emotion as a guide for what to say and when. Emotion is information to let you know how you feel. However, emotion is not a guide for how to express you. Love and wisdom best inform communication's messages. Use wisdom and love to ease toxic emotions; and then use them to express yourself.

THE SECRET POWER OF WORD

So powerful-
IT can crush a heart or heal it.
IT can shame a soul or liberate it.
IT can shatter dreams or energize them.

IT can obstruct connection or invite it.
IT can create defenses or melt them.
We can choose to use words wisely.

Tasha M. Gooden

The primary purpose of communication is to let other people know who you are, and how you can best connect with each other. Using communication skills, you can offer love, advice, support, and everything you wish to express. Others can learn how to best connect with you. Communication is a wonderful vehicle from which mutual respect can evolve.

Productive communication requires several skills. Some of these skills are learned in families and social groups. However, we also may learn destructive communication patterns which can wreak havoc on relationships. It is important to be aware of which patterns are destructive versus which are productive to relationships.

YOUR INTERNAL DELIVERY STYLE

I message" are the opposite of "you messages". "I message" help you to be heard, understood, and responded to. "I message" need to be clear. An "I message" is a statement about what is happening in you, what you think, how you feel, what you want, and so on. By making and "I message", you are taking responsibility for letting another know your wishes, wants, experiences, and expectations.

"You messages" are usually statements about the person being spoken to. "You messages" are often judgments, evaluations, or accusations. "You messages" usually trigger defensiveness and get in the way of healthy communication. They provoke the other person to argue with you before listening to you. When in a disagreement, Avoid "you messages".

Examples of "You Messages", changed to "I messages":

"You never make enough time to talk." --- "I need some time to talk about ..."

"You should care more about ....." --- "I'm concerned about... Do you care about this too? I feel alone."

"You aren't cooperating" --- "I feel alone. Can we talk about cooperating more?"

"You don't make me a priority" --- "I feel hurt; I don't feel like I am a priority."

"You are selfish to travel so much." --- "I am afraid I am losing you when you are gone so much."

"Everybody Messages" also get in the way of healthy communication. They are usually vague generalizations. Using them is an avoidance of being open and direct.

Examples: "Everybody feels that..." "Everyone knows it is not good to..." "It is impossible for anybody to..."

Awareness of Destructive Communication Patterns

While building productive communication skills, it is important to avoid destructive communication traps. The following communication patterns will cause harm and destruction. Be aware of them and avoid them.

- blaming the other person for problems. Accusations can produce defensiveness, argument, and insincere apologies

- name calling; putting the other person down; attacking the other person rather than attacking the problem

- aggression or physical abuse

- not treating the other person as an equal

- not staying <u>focused</u> on the issue, you are discussing

- making threats

- withdrawing from the discussion because you are angry (on the other hand, it is healthy communication to say you are taking a 'time-out' if you feel too emotional to be productive)

- being indirect; not saying what you mean and talking around it

- being disrespectful, rude, thoughtless, or attacking

- arguing with the other person's feelings; invalidating the other's feelings; saying "You shouldn't feel that way" (a "You message")

- 'mind reading'- telling the other person what they are thinking or feeling; telling them why they behave as they do; not listening to their thoughts, feelings, and understanding of his/herself

- talking too loudly or making the message complicated

- one-upping the other person

- the 'Win-Lose Trap': This is when someone is trying to 'win' or prove the other person 'wrong', rather than communicating thoughts and feelings. Ask yourself,

- "Do I want to share my thoughts and feelings, and to learn theirs? Or do I want to prove my position is right, no matter the cost to the relationship? What is my intention?

- Do I want us to understand each other? The 'Win-Lose Trap' promotes distance and conflict; healthy communication promotes understanding and closeness.

Assertiveness

Asserting yourself with others helps them learn more about who you are. It draws love and respect to you. At the same time, it protects you from being drawn into others passive and/or aggressive attachments to you. As you develop your unique style of asserting yourself in the world, your awareness, love, and respect for yourself deepen. The more you know yourself, the more assertive you will become, creating a wonderful feedback loop. At first, being assertive may feel uncomfortable and strange. But soon, the benefits will bring <u>peace</u> and strength to your self- expression.

Assertiveness is a healthy way of relating. It is an open and honest way of expressing yourself. Unlike aggression (which uses force and opposition) and passivity (which tends to create misunderstanding and confusion), assertiveness allows for cooperation, clarity, and the <u>freedom</u> to be yourself. When being assertive, you expose yourself to a degree that is in your best interest. This expression may be verbal or non-verbal.

Requirements of Assertiveness:
- be aware of your intentions, feelings, and ideas

- directly express your intentions, <u>feelings</u>, and ideas
- when making decisions, consider the needs of both self and others
- look directly at the other person(s)
- be responsible for your choices
- stay calm
- give yourself permission to make mistakes
- let go of self-judgment / see yourself with eyes of love
- be responsible (deal directly) with the outcomes of your mistakes/errors. This leads to your increased knowledge, growth, and <u>wisdom</u>.
- be responsible for your feelings, beliefs, and opinions
- be responsible for your timing and expression
- be honest when you do not want to give and/or receive help
- be honest about your intentions
- be honest with others when you are upset with them
- stand-up for yourself and your rights
- respect the rights of others
- encourage yourself and others

Benefits of Assertiveness:

- awareness to meet needs
- increased hope for the ability to meet your goals
- the freedom to decide when to explain or justify your behavior, and when not to
- the freedom to change your mind, including times when others may want to hold you to a position
- the ability to set your boundaries
- the ability to say 'No' out of love
- not feeling guilty or responsible for the other person's reaction
- self- trust and respect - often leading to the trust and respect of others
- self confidence
- the freedom to admit you do not know something
- a sense of internal peace

Aggression is NOT Assertiveness! Aggression is a way of communicating that acts against others, often attempting to accomplish goals by hurting others.

Characteristics of aggression:

- demanding others cooperate with your goals

- dominating and discouraging others
- telling others what to do, without their permission
- controlling situations, and controlling other people
- expressing needs, feelings, and ideas, without being open to the different needs, feelings, and ideas of others
- using force
- being judgmental
- being oppositional
- justifying your unfair treatment of others
- defensiveness
- refusal to compromise

Outcomes of aggression:
- humiliating others
- feeling misunderstood, frustrated, bitter, and angry
- feeling alone and guilty
- confusion
- isolation, as others create distance from you to protect themselves
- feeling rejected

Passivity is NOT Assertiveness! Passivity is communicating in a way that does not take care of oneself.

Characteristics of passive communication:

- dishonest expression of your thoughts and feelings
- Avoiding responsibility for self-care (Even when you are caring for others, it is your primary responsibility to care for yourself. If you do not, others may feel pressured to care for you, clouding their freedom to say 'No' to you.)
- ignoring your rights, and allowing others to ignore them
- being indirect
- blaming others for decisions in your life
- allowing others to make decisions for you

Outcomes of passivity:

- feeling disappointed
- feeling anxious, fearful, tired, and/or depressed
- feeling used and/or resentful
- having a negative attitude about yourself
- feeling helpless and misunderstood
- physical symptoms

Assert yourself! Show the world who you truly are!! The world will benefit!!!

Validation and Listening

What does it mean to validate someone's communication with you?

- to validate is to give value to the other person's message
- what they say is valuable because it is their point of view
- it is valuable because it teaches you about them
- your agreement with their message is only one way to validate
    - you can <u>disagree</u> with the other's point of view and still validate
- you give their message attention
- you show respect for their communication with you
- you acknowledge their message is what they feel and/or think
- you listen, without arguing (later, you may state your different point of view)

Research has shown the amount of validation does not predict relationship health.... BUT, the amount of invalidation is a factor in predicting relationship Problems.

Active Listening helps to provide validation of the other person's message. Active listening involves the following:

- get ready to listen by looking at the other person
- watch and listen to the person
- listen for ideas and feelings
- pay attention to the message
- take the other person's viewpoint into consideration (even if you disagree)
- do not interrupt
- do not finish the other person's sentences

An example of **Active Listening** creating validation:

- Speaker- "I wish you spent time with me more often. I am hurt that our evenings tend to be time apart."
- Listener- "You feel hurt when I don't spend more time with you in the evening? I guess I knew that. However, I didn't give it enough thought and attention before." (Do NOT say, "You shouldn't feel hurt. Don't take it personally.")

Reflective Listening is a specific form of **Active Listening.**

Reflective Listening:

- Is a skill to promote further validation in communication?
- Involves reiterating what is heard, to check whether the sender's message is accurately understood.

- Is like using a mirror, informing both parties about whether the listener heard the message correctly.
- Helps to clarify what the speaker is saying.
- Let's the speaker know the listener values (validation) understanding the message.

Here is how **Reflective Listening** works:
- 1 - the speaker gives a message
- 2 - the receiver / listener paraphrases (saying it in your own words) the message back to the speaker.

"What I hear you saying is..."

"Do you mean...?"

"Let me see if what I heard is what you are saying..."

- *The speaker may also ask for clarification: "What do you hear me saying?"*
- The receiver / listener asks if this is the intended message (you are checking to find out if what you heard is what the speaker meant) if the paraphrase isn't what the speaker meant; the speaker repeats the message until it is heard clearly

This may take several back and forth interchanges. Words do not always relay a message as clearly as it is in our thoughts. There is a message sent by the speaker, and a message received by the listener. These messages are not always the same. Reflective listening allows the listener to feed back the message heard, to get the speaker to clarify whether the message was heard correctly and in full. This immediate feedback and clarification avoid misunderstandings based on natural assumptions the listeners make about messages heard.

Reflective Listening is an important skill when there is a conflict, a problem to solve, and/or indirect communication. Take care not to overuse this skill, as it can lose effectiveness with overuse. However, be sure to use it any time you assume you know what someone is meaning to say.

Create healthy new patterns. Ask your loved one what you can do to let them know you are listening and wanting to understand his/her message to you. Discuss what it is like for him/her when thinking you are not listening. Discuss what he/she does when not feeling listened to or understood. This information can be helpful to both of you for identifying future discussions in which you need to listen more. Create the relationship you desire.

The Power of Love

Use love to embrace the other person's desire to communicate with you. Remember, communication is for the purpose of building healthy relationships; it is not for the purpose of controlling another. As the listener, it is SO important to use this time to LEARN the message of the speaker. If necessary, pretend you are a stranger, trying to understand what this person is expressing. This is NOT the time to judge or correct the message, or to interject your own thoughts and/or position. NOW is the time to assert your peace into the relationship.

Every Door has a Heart Beat

Connect my headphones into your heart.
Hear the beat of your blood,
Feel the flow of your love.
Let us listen together,

As love's harmony manifests in our lives.

The way you express yourself teaches the world who you are. This expression has a major impact on the quality of your connections with others. Quality connections create productive discussions, resolutions, relationship patterns, and more. Destructive connections create destructive outcomes (e.g. misunderstandings, arguments, fractured relationships, unhealthy patterns). Take an inventory of your intentions, thoughts, and emotions. Intend to express yourself in ways that promote mutually beneficial connections. Choose goals aligned with healthy connections.

On this page you will find information about the following communication skills:

95

- **Choosing Intentions, Thoughts, and Emotions to Best Drive Your Expressions**
- **Maintaining Focus**
- **Attention and Clear Expressions**
- **Respectful Disagreement**

Manifestation

Choosing Intentions, Thoughts, and Emotions to Best Drive Your Expressions

Your thoughts about another person (their actions, words, appearance, demographics, etc....) determine how you interact with him/her. If your thoughts of others come from your love, self-control, and self-confidence, you will tend to interact in ways that create a sense of satisfaction and purpose. However, if you choose thoughts that produce fear, opposition, or anxiety in you, your interactions will most likely reflect this and create a sense of less control in the situation.

In order to have thoughts and emotions that create healthy interactions, intend to see others through eyes of love. Know they too desire to be in loving, healthy, productive connections. If the other person does not appear loving, think of their love as hidden (by fear, resentment, confusion, etc....). Connect to your sense of internal peace (despite the level of chaos in the environment). Your emotions are dependent on your perspective (thoughts, attitudes, and judgments) and your ability to connect with internal peace. Choose thoughts of self- confidence, and self-control; choose thoughts of love for yourself and the other person. Then connect with the other person to the degree you are able to extend loving intentions. Your ability to extend love does not depend on the other's ability to reciprocate. Your ability to extend love depends on your ability to anchor your expression in loving intentions for connection.

Focusing on *your responsibilities* in the communication (e.g. honesty, assertiveness, reason, and productivity) brings you confidence and clarity. However, if you focus on what you cannot control (e.g. the other's attitude, perspective, judgment, mood, honesty), you may miss out on potential opportunity for a constructive interaction.

You are responsible for how you see the world (your perspective) and your attitude towards it. These responsibilities have an enormous influence on your interactions. Practice the following recommendations:

- Look for peace and unity: you will find it, even when others do not. Expose it through your interactions and example (e.g. through anecdotal information and through your style of interacting). Value compassion, honesty, confidence, assertiveness, and peace for healthier, stronger, more honest connections - despite challenging interactions.

- Work to understand the other's situation and reasoning. You will have more information in the exchange.

- If you judge the other and are not open to understanding his/her reasoning, you will have a faulty understanding of the information being expressed to you. This can leave you feeling confused, alone, and/or separate.

- Do not spend energy trying to control the thoughts of someone who does not want your perspective; even if you believe you know what is best for him/her. Be careful - what you try to control can control you.

- Reason and <u>peace</u> are more <u>powerful</u> than aggression and confusion. If you do not accept this, you will fear the aggression and confusion of others. Fear can limit and control you, often leading to a self -fulfilling prophesy. Your fear can fuel aggression and confusion in your own expression.

- Connect with your internal sense of peace by releasing unhealthy attitudes (blame, resentment, judgment, etc.). If you hold onto thoughts of being harmed or not loved in ways you desire, you block your own sense of peace. Even if you must create <u>boundaries</u> to maintain your safety (physical or emotional), your heart can hold deep love for the other.

- Intend to <u>accept yourself</u> as you are - and as you grow. Discover and embrace encouraging beliefs about yourself. As you learn about your unique identity, free of judgment and measurement, you discover your healthy/true self. As your identity unfolds, your self-expression connects you to others in ways that are supportive and empowering.

You will create the relationships you desire.
One must allow awareness into the infinite context
of your life.
Allow awareness to create an unfolding through
you.
Allow the power of love, to bring forth your greatest
offering.

Tasha M. Gooden

One must be affectionate, caring, loving, and warm increase healthy connections in relationships. While connection is often desired, it is also often feared. Ironically, fear creates unhealthy connections which are the very type of connection being feared. In this way, unhealthy connections are formed and reinforced over time, situations, and generations.

On this page, you will find information about the following communication skills:

- *Identifying and Resolving Fears preventing closeness in relationships*
- *Giving Compliments and Verbal Affection*
- *Communicating Feelings*

Identifying and Resolving Fears in Relationships

Your feelings are a gift, bringing you information about yourself. Without this information (whether comfortable or uncomfortable), your experiences would lack an awareness and experience of your inner self. Feelings help expose the depth of who you are, beyond your thoughts alone.
While thoughts create feelings, feelings can exist after thoughts fade. Thus, your feelings are like a record of your subjective experiences.
Bring awareness to your feelings to increase your clarity, choice, and creation of who you are and where you are heading on your amazing journey!

Feelings are information. They do not tell you what *to do*. They do tell you your *emotional temperature* in a given situation. If feelings are ignored, the information they could provide is not available and ignorance results. The feelings themselves do not evaporate. Feelings are messages from you, to you. Ignoring them can result in intensified messages in your own unconscious effort towards self-understanding. Increasing emotional discomfort may be an indication you are

100

not paying enough attention to the information feelings are offering. Or the discomfort may indicate you are giving attention to the feelings, yet not acting in your best interest.

When we experience *hurt, rejection,* and/or *loss,* we may develop an unhealthy emotional attachment to the experience. Believing future emotions are dependent on present experience creates an unhealthy dependence on (attachment to) the experience. Do not depend on the emotion in the experience. Instead, utilize thoughtful consideration: determine what to take from the experience into the future (lessons, new boundaries, facts, a clearer understanding c). As we go forward in time, *unhealthy emotional attachments to the past* can be thought of as emotional scar tissue. The scar tissue blocks healthy connection to the present. Emotional attachments to the past create a skewed perception of the present, potentially promoting isolation from current relationship opportunities. Thus, misguided perceptions are self- fulfilling, as one feels additional hurt, rejection, and/or loss due to current **emotional isolation**. Emotional attachments to the past block emotional connections in the present.

The more one perceives emotional isolation, the more **emotional scar tissue** builds, and the more fear of vulnerability operates. An underlying fear of **vulnerability, helplessness,** or **loss of control** may project into the world as an attitude of **toughness** or **over control**.

Some signs of emotional attachment:
- believing present happiness is dependent on history
- ruminating about the past
- investing emotional energy into the past
- clinging to the thought the past should be different than it is
- choosing feelings to author memories
- letting feelings set the course of an experience
- letting feelings dictate actions, rather than using thoughtful consideration from a clear perspective

Loving feelings towards others can be covered up by unhealthy emotional attachments. You may be so angry at someone it is difficult to feel love for the person. **To break through unhealthy attachment**, figure out what you are angry about. **Consider how you will let the past effect the present.** Unhealthy attachments to the past can be due to believing your happiness in the present was dependent/is dependent on someone/something external. However, people and events merely trigger what exists within you. Knowing this can reduce unhealthy beliefs about experiences and increase the power to see meaning in experiences. You can't erase **painful memories**; but you can decide whether to define yourself as a **helpless** victim of the past, or as a person able to let go of **dis-ease**.

Events of the past do not have to interrupt your happiness your present. Your perception of your experience is your emotional compass. Don't choose to see yourself as helpless. Choose to accept what happened, accept you can't change it, and know you can learn from it. Give meaning and purpose to your past experiences, to be able to see your whole life as meaningful. **Free_yourself** from **emotional investment against the people** you think are responsible for pain in your life (including any emotions you hold against yourself). As you do this, you further a sense of control for your life today. Let go of **resentment, guilt, accusation**, and **blame** attached to the past, to allow you the freedom, energy, wisdom, and power to **form healthy relationships** in the present.

If you believe expressing closeness makes you less of a person, you will fear closeness. Thinking "men have to be tough" ... "softness is weak"... "Men are logical, women are emotional" creates unreasonable perceptions and expectations, encouraging you to shut down feelings. These beliefs, which are sometimes called " unspoken rules," ignore the reality that men and women experience the same feelings. Do you ever think this way? Do others in your relationships have these beliefs? Awareness is a place to start healing from misperceptions.

You block yourself from expressing closeness when you think **"I have to be right"** ... **"I have to be one-upped"** ... "I have to prove you are wrong or bad." These thoughts come from a **competitive attitude.** A healthy attitude strives to make the relationship empowering for both people. If you are afraid to admit your limitations, or if you have to have the only "right" answer, you fear closeness.

Do you avoid expressing feelings when you do not know what the response will be? You will fear closeness if you do not know you can cope with the discomfort which may arise from responses to your openness and honesty. Being open and honest are strengths. When you tell your truth, no matter the response, your truth is strength in and of itself.

Communicating Feelings

Communication is an expression of 'awareness' and 'experience'. 'Experience' is how you are affected by what has happened or is happening. 'Awareness' is your recognition of your thoughts, feelings, bodily sensations, images, and memories. The more you are aware of yourself, the more you are able to express yourself clearly to others, and to recognize similar experiences of others.

Feelings are complex reactions involving physical and psychological responses. Thoughts have chemical responses. These chemicals are experienced through various parts of the body. Hence, we notice a feeling correlating with a physical response. Thinking someone is about to attack you may produce adrenaline (needed for expending physical energy), often creating a fight or flight experience. Thoughts of past abuse may create a tightening of muscles, experienced as anger or fear; increased sweat may correlate with fear; relaxation with relief; and abdominal distress with resentment. Changes in the body are often noticed before changes in mood are identified. In this way, the body may give clues before the feelings are obvious.

Feelings can alert us to danger, helping us survive and stay healthy. Some feelings function as indicators of our physical, mental, emotional, and social health.

Feelings are created by thoughts about people, places, things, and ideas. When thoughts are unhealthy, uncomfortable feelings may form. Many thoughts, opinions, and points of view are learned from life experiences. When we aren't getting what we want, we experience uncomfortable feelings. To feel better, reevaluate strategies or priorities. It may be best to change the thought, opinion, and point of view to meet goals in a healthier way (to achieve a new

105

perspective, increased acceptance, decreased judgment, a life lesson, a higher goal, a new insight). Be empowered: thoughts can create feelings; thoughts can be changed.

Thoughts and Feeling are like thermostats.

Thoughts set our attitude to create our feelings. Feelings give us information about our state of being.

To best communicate feelings:

- **Be aware of what you are feeling and the thoughts creating your feelings.**

- Take time to be clear in your mind regarding the goal(s) of your communication.

- If needed: clarify goals with a friend, write your goals, role play the conversation before having it.

- Provide a clear expression of your feelings and thoughts. (Words are symbols, helping others understand your awareness and experience.)

  - For example, saying "I'm feeling upset right now, and I would like you to listen to me" communicates both a feeling and a request.

- *Do not assume another person knows how you feel or what you want.*

- It is your **responsibility** to express yourself.

If you are feeling angry or frustrated, express yourself to the other person. This creates an opportunity to discuss and resolve potential issues. Before doing this, know your goal(s) for the discussion. If the other person will not cooperate in resolving issues, express your thoughts and feelings to someone who can help you <u>resolve your feelings of anger</u> and frustration.

It is often difficult to express uncomfortable feelings (sadness, anger frustration, confusion, disappointment, etc.). Typically, people are not encouraged to express these feelings. When not recognized, expressed, and acknowledged in productive ways, these feelings can grow from the inside out, forcing expression in unproductive ways at inopportune times. Feelings held inside may *seem* to lie dormant. However, they can act like a poison to self-awareness and experience. Ignored feelings can obstruct your ability to think, feel, and express clearly.

Expressions of feelings may be met with invalidating responses: "You shouldn't feel that way," or "Don't tell me feelings like that". No matter what you predict the response will be, it is your responsibility to express yourself in most situations. (Some exceptions: situations that may become abusive; or, when the other person has made it clear they are not interested in knowing more about you).

Stay aware of your feelings. Do not try to push them away, cover them up, or pretend they do not exist. They are information for you, about you. No matter how uncomfortable they may be, feelings are a gift, a way of <u>knowing yourself</u> more <u>deeply</u>. For others who care about you, your feelings are a precious piece of information about how to connect with you in a more intimate way. Becoming more aware of yourself and others leads to increased acceptance and caring. You cannot avoid all <u>conflicts</u> and disagreements; but you can resolve them in a more productive and loving way.

Feelings are not to be argued about or judged. Feelings are indicators/barometers to be recognized as helpful information. To argue about a feeling is like arguing about the reading of a thermometer. When one person does not accept another's feelings as real, the result is usually unnecessary conflict.

Feelings are indicators of whether needs and desires are being met in healthy ways. Feelings do NOT inform you how to act in a situation. For example, you may want the other person to agree with your point of view. He/she may see your point of view as naive. In response, you may feel hurt and distant from the other person, wanting to avoid him/her (potential action). Your feelings, like a **thermometer**, let you know you are uncomfortable. Your feelings also tempt you to be distant from the other person (potential action). Remember, your feelings are the thermometer, not the decision maker. Do not use feelings alone to decide your actions. Your mind is the thermostat...Your mind must decide the best course of action, using the feeling (thermometer) as one indicator of the environment. The mind must see from a larger context than simply the feeling. The mind must also consider the goal of connection, understanding, and more. Thoughtful consideration reveals it is necessary to interact with the other person in order to determine what is wrong, how you both feel and think, and how to solve the problem. In this situation, **your feelings give information about an unmet need or desire; they are not useful in deciding what to do to solve the problem**. In this situation, using your feelings alone to decide what to do (be distant) could make the problem worse.

Expressing feelings can help you:
- sooth uncomfortable feelings
- gain greater self-control
- increase closeness in the relationship

Not expressing feelings can cause you:
- more intense and confused feelings
- misunderstanding in the relationships
- physical problems
- feelings of helplessness and isolation

Your feelings are crucial information about you.

Without this information, you would lack an awareness of your inner self - the depth of who you are beyond your thoughts alone. Remember while thoughts create feelings, the feelings stay beyond the thoughts. In each moment, choose your thoughts wisely, in order to create healthy feelings. Feelings are like a record of how you have perceived experiences. Be aware of your thoughts and feelings to increase clarity, choice, and creation of who you are and where you are heading on your amazing journey!

Giving Compliments and Verbal Affection

Genuine compliments improve closeness in relationships. Compliments let others know you support them. If you tend to have a critical frame of mind, complimenting others can help you let go of critical thoughts.

Look for opportunities to create compliments:

- Notice behaviors you appreciate. Encourage them to continue by complimenting the person. One of the best ways to let someone know you are pleased with changes is by clearly verbalizing what you like.

- Notice a small action creating a healthy connection. Tell the person.

- "Catch" someone doing something well. Tell the person.

Stay Aware:

In close relationships:

- You can have a strong **influence** on others' self-esteem.

- **Notice** ways you benefit from the atmosphere of the relationship.

- **Praise** the qualities and actions of others contributing to a healthy atmosphere.

- **Compliment** changes in the present, without referring to what you didn't prefer in the past. For example, say "Your words are so kind", not "You're finally so much kinder than you use to be".

- If you think of someone in a negative way, **notice** a way they bring support to your life. **Tell** them about it.

- Give **surprise compliments**: a card, letter, or picture expressing appreciation.

- Others have the right to opinions different from yours. They also have the right to express criticism. When criticized, respond **nondefensively**.

- **Practice** using the phrases - "I love you," "I'm sorry", and "Thank you."

With yourself:

- **Notice** destructive thoughts and **replace** them with productive thoughts.

- **Give** yourself compliments.

- **Value** accomplishments you may consider small - they are more significant than you know!

- In situations where you are tempted to express yourself with poor communication, **stop and consider** at least two other ways to communicate.

- In rough moments, **remember** <u>assertiveness</u>.

- **Encourage** yourself to stay with changes you want to make, even if they are difficult, awkward, and frightening at first.

To increase the sense of safety in relationships, <u>create</u> an environment where:

- people feel free to talk about feelings

- all feelings are acceptable

- everyone is encouraged to experience a high sense of self-worth

- all issues are acceptable

- people are more important than performance

- laughter and joy are encouraged

- the atmosphere is relaxed

- each person is responsible for his/her own actions

- people have energy

- growth and success are celebrated

- all members acknowledge existing stress, and work through it together
- people feel loved
- unity exists - differences are accepted
- respectful criticism is offered
- there is a sense of trust

Over time, as you approach communication more effectively, you will be more able and confident expressing yourself. Choose how you connect with others. ***You are connected, so create the connections you desire!***

When we see through eyes of pure Love, we are Free to love freely.

We must be willing to trust love. Love brings forth clarity to see life through a pure heart - Free of darkness, shadows, blame, resentment, or any clouds that dim love's light. By trusting love, fear is dissolved. Freedom to live confidently in love's purity becomes a reality...not just a concept. As we live in this Freedom, it is shared with those around us who are also ready to trust love's power. This Freedom is exposed; it cannot be imposed.

As we trust love, we are able to put aside any selfish agenda. This selfish agenda is what we become Free from! We are Free to allow only love's creation to be manifested in and through us. Humility shows us that we do not get credit for what love create through us. Better than getting any credit, as we allow love to create through us, we are created by love... We become more pure love in the world. We shine brighter. In truth, love is all that we are. We swim in love: we are love. We submit to love. Only love is stable. Only love is safe. Only love deepens our sense of who we honestly are and want to be. To choose to submit to anything else creates a distraction appearing as a prison. In that prison, we are not Free to see the only honest choice to make is love. Do not submit to distraction's illusion of prison; submit to love's Freedom.

An illusion is when the mind chooses thoughts that put Love in a false prison. Do we ever use our thoughts to judge a person? Notice that when we judge someone who is promoting confusion and destructiveness, we become confused and destructive. In this way, we steal our own love, mercy, and compassion for that person. We take away our Freedom to love. In a relationship, do we fear that we are being accused or attacked, and so defend ourselves with verbal, physical, or emotional aggression? Fear creates misunderstanding and a skewed sense of truth. It limits what we allow love to do in and through us. We must bypass fear and judgment. We can attack the problem by not attacking the other person. How much do we trust love's wisdom, despite our fear induced limitations?

Just as we must not condemn others, we must not condemn the self. Freedom does not have room for self-condemnation. Self-condemnation steals time, energy, and emotions that are to be used by love. Love always exists. It has no limit. The more we allow it to use us, the more we are empowered by it. We are Free to allow love to manifest and <u>create </u>our lives.

Love's path brings Freedom, but it does not necessarily bring physical comfort and safety. Comfort and safety may occur; but until everyone submits to love's truths, results of fear will impact this world. Expect love to be misunderstood. The Freedom to love cannot be taken away. Beware: the degree of focus on fear's destruction (<u>fear in self, or in others</u>) is the degree love's power is made vulnerable. Thus, when fear is revealed, respond with love's power. Shine the <u>light</u> of love so brightly that fear's darkness cannot hide. By showing others the power of love, their fears can be transcended.

We are Free to the degree we trust love. When we dissolve illusions of limits to our Love, we are Free to know love, no matter what. A life of love is immersed in Freedom and truth. In reality, love is not given or received. <u>Love</u> is the Freedom we swim in. Through love, the heart is Free to imagine, create, and manifest its infinite truth. Through love, we see the <u>Divinity</u> of All. We are Free to grow in strength and power, putting our minds and emotions into joy and possibilities.

Seeing through the Light of love, you will know protection and joy. This seeing provides endurance to continue in seemingly impossible situations. It provides wisdom to understand that circumstance is only part of the picture; and the total picture may be paradoxical to what appeared to be true (e.g., a "Blessing in disguise").

"Love is patient, love is kind. ... Love rejoices with the Truth.

It always protects, always trusts, always hopes, always perseveres. Love never fails. ...

For we know in part, ...but when perfection comes, the imperfect disappears....

Now I know in part, then I shall know fully, even as I am fully known."

1 Corinthians 13:4, 6-10, 12

Look with eyes of love into your life, without judgment, trusting the desires in your heart are coming into fruition. Whether you are in a time of trouble or joy, look through a lens of love not fear. Look beyond the limited context of physical circumstance. Broaden your context to see a world illuminated in love's Light. See the grand scheme of all possibilities yet to be chosen from. Let your choosing be inspired and guided by love. These choices will bring forth clarity and evidence for increased understanding of the larger Truth. Don't limit your life to anything less.

Love's Light is Honest:

When you find yourself in the midst of a dark night, it may seem all light has disappeared. But you know the truth---Light makes darkness disappear. If you think you need more light than you see, don't allow fearful thoughts to darken your perception. Fear's lies are blinding. The truth is you have all the Light you need. Love's Light can illuminate the best next step to take. Love's Light is always turned on. Shutting your eyes in fear does not make the Light disappear? Open your eyes! Each moment you are willing to trust love; you step deeper into love's greater context of _peace_ and _harmony_.

When stars shine Light, their energy radiates throughout the solar system. When you radiate your love Light in and through your life, this _power_ reaches all the lives you are connected to (All of Life!). But when you allow anything to interrupt love from flowing in and through your life, illusions of darkness and powerlessness will appear. Apparent darkness is a signal to you to become more aware of Light. Light is always available to you.

Trust when Light enters darkness, you will see the purpose for the apparent darkness. Love's potential is beyond what you know here and now. Become aware of the limit of what you know...your darkness. This darkness is not to be feared; it is to be embraced as a sign to look out further into the unknown until you see your Light.

You may have graduated to a new horizon of understanding. It may take time to adjust to the new frequency of Light available to you. Consider this: when the moon is between the earth and the sun, we cannot see the Light of the sun on the moon at night. We call this the New Moon. Have you outgrown an old understanding of the world? Are your old ideas blocking love's Light from illuminating a greater context for your life? Is there darkness revealing it is time for your New Moon/New Horizon? You may see a dark and lonely night look further to see a night full of bright stars. Looking further brings greater understanding. Greater understanding transforms the experience of darkness and suffering into purpose and wisdom. Understand who you are in a larger context. Transcend the darkness! Let greater trust shine its energy into your life. Reflect this Light back onto your life. This is your FULL Moon.

One of Love's Lights is Trust. Sometimes you can't see what you think you need to see. At these times, what you really need is trust to light your way. When you plant a seed, you don't demand there be evidence of it growing in order to trust it is, or evidence of blossoms to believe it will bear fruit. Time may be a factor in evidence coming forward. When you don't see the evidence you think you need, there may be an unknown factor involved.

Identify any factors (e.g., fear, distrust, judgment, etc.) keeping you from trust (love's Light). Do not put your trust in these factors. They limit your ability to trust love, when you can't see the fruit of love yet. Realize: **the ability to see with trust (love's Light) is the greatest fruit.**

Look out at the star Light; understand your world is so much bigger than you can see or imagine. The sunrise is beautiful - not because we get to see it all at once, but because the earth slowly turns, revealing its' radiant Light to us in its' own perfect timing. The shift from darkness to Light is a time of waiting. Don't get lost in suffering or stuck in despair. Darkness is seen when we are not yet able to see the larger context. The larger context includes Light. As we wait in trust, we can feel this radiant Light of love rising up in us, using us to shine Light for all to see the larger picture. We can offer patience, grace, hope, wisdom, tenderness, compassion, forgiveness, and much more to the world. In this Divine space, your life becomes a Light to illuminate infinite possibilities for all to know the love of self, of others, and of unity.

Love's Light Expands and Purifies Your Vision:

When you think you are having a crisis, do you wonder how it may change your life in ways that evolve you? Do you consider how this moment may transform and amplify your service and love in the world? Or do you limit yourself to suffering, as if it is the end of the story? Using love's Light, integrate the present experience with the evolution which is still <u>hidden</u>. Harmonize your physical knowledge with spiritual knowledge for a greater context. This will give you a more thorough understanding of your life.

Why do we have to be like the caterpillar? Why do we have stages in life when we don't appear able to fly; when we have to ingest every bit of healthy encouragement just to function; when we feel heavy hearts; when we can't see beyond what is near to us? Being a caterpillar is the necessary nourishing stage of eating and growing for the butterfly. For humans, we eat reality to become humble. (Love's power cannot operate without humility.) We have to develop humility, wisdom, and courage. We must learn the limits of our brains' perspectives. We learn of our hearts' love Light. We are <u>free</u> from the traps of <u>anger</u>, passivity, or fear - no matter the circumstance. We experience the power that comes from an even deeper understanding of love's Light in what appeared to be dark places. When we depend on love to illuminate each beneficial step in life, we evolve through all circumstances. We become butterflies.

The butterfly flies and expands life. It creates life, and it plays with other butterflies. It colonizes new areas with fresh plants and migrates long distances to escape freezing winters. The shift in context of life from caterpillar to butterfly is the responsibility of each of us. You can live and die as a limited caterpillar, or you can evolve to fly as a beautiful butterfly. Let your heart's Light inform and transform you. Create and play; colonize new areas with fresh ideas; expand the territory of your love; escape isolation. Be wise; let your light shine on your courage. You have more light and courage than you know.

All people are on a journey in life. Some are more like caterpillars; some are more like butterflies. ALL are necessary to the process of creating unity and harmony. When you encounter someone, who seems to limit your ability to fly, it is actually your judgment limiting you. Get out of your way. Let go of seeing limit; see and seize this opportunity. Shine love's Light onto the other person. They may be in the necessary eating and growing stage (caterpillar). Give them encouragement, not judgment. Be patient as they crawl. Someday they may join you and play with you in flight. For now, you live in two different worlds (crawling and flying), having two different vantage points and understandings of world context. Remember that to someone else, *you* appear to be a caterpillar. Thankfully, they are a butterfly who is already full of wisdom and patience, encouraging you. NOW, evolve into the wiser butterfly.

Love' and Wisdom creates Confidence:
Put Love's Light into Your Eyes,
Love's Sound into Your Ears,

Love's Taste onto Your Tongue,

Love's Touch onto Your Skin,

Love's Fragrance into Your Nose.

Interpret the Whole World Through Your New Senses!!!

The world, seen through the eyes of love, is a different world than seen through the eyes of the ego. The ego contains fear, force, arrogance, and limitation. It sees a world of darkness. Trust love's wisdom and Spirit. Trust in the existence of a larger context. You will sense peace beyond your understanding. Love is dependable, honest, humble, courageous, and has access to more truth than the brain can understand. Love's strength is powerful and gentle.

"Rejoice in the Spirit always. Again, I will say, rejoice!
Let your gentleness be known to all. The Spirit is at hand.
Be anxious for nothing, but in everything by prayer and supplication,
with thanksgiving, let your requests be made known to God.
The Peace of God, which surpasses all understanding,
will guard your hearts and your minds"
Philippians 4:4-7

This transcendent peace supersedes any other focus for peace. It takes priority over physical peace, emotional peace, financial peace, and any other subordinate peace. Although this peace surpasses your understanding, it can become your primary experience in every situation. Great peace already exists within you; it needs only to be discovered. Let love's Light shine into your understanding of who you are. See yourself through eyes of pure love. The Spirit of love is alive in you and Light's your way. To understand your life in the larger the context, understand information and circumstance without utilizing fear. Let love's Light wash away anxiety and despair, and shine Light into darkness.

This is the message which we have heard from God and declare to you, that God's Spirit is Light and in this Spirit is no darkness at all.
1 John 1:5

Wisdom takes the bits of information our physical senses provide and inputs them into the larger context. The larger the context, the more Light required to see it. If you shine a flashlight, you will see into the darkness. If you turn on an overhead light, you can light up a room. If the sun is shining, lesser lights are dissolved into the illumination and the darkness is no longer a factor. Your physical senses are like the flashlight, light bulb, night vision goggles, or any inorganic technology. They are useful but limited.

Love's Light is like the sun, revealing all...full of power, illumination, and eternal energy.

Trust love's Light to bring the desires of your heart (your purposes) to fruition. Your desires and purposes go beyond what your mind can fathom. One purpose fulfilled leads to another. Using love, to determine each step, provides the safety you crave. As <u>love</u> is expended, it grows. Do not use fear... as fear is expended, it also grows. Use love's wisdom to choose your steps safely.

Love's Light Dissolves Fear:

What you believe you see determines your attitude, perspective, and behavior. If you believe someone or something is dangerous, you are vulnerable to fear and anxiety. While it is important to know what our senses tell us about the environment, it is important to know how to understand the context and greater picture.

When you see others as problematic or dangerous, look further. Shine love's Light into their darkness to see your safety beyond their impact on you. **Love's impact is greater than the impact of anything else...even when you cannot see the impact with your physical senses.** When you know this, you have internal safety, no matter the external situation. To have peace in your mind and heart, see beyond errors, faults, finances, politics, prejudices. Let love shine through you because of what is in YOUR heart. Do not be dependent on another's agenda. Your Divine love is needed in the world. Do not let your ability to love be stifled by hate from you or for you. Be filled with love's Light. In all circumstances, trust the <u>wisdom</u> of love. Feel into your heart to know how to be fearless and loving...to know how to respond in circumstances that appear to be overwhelming when seen with eyes of fear. When you watch media, when you see drama, when your own life feels overwhelming, you need to know what to trust. Go into your heart and find love. Trust love's wisdom THERE.

Do not put any faith in fear. Fear limits love's Light. Expect love to protect you. Love's Light is your protection against darkness. Through a lens of fear, life feels pointless, efforts useless, motivations wasted- darkness soaking everything. What you know is true of love (that it heals all, that it protects you, that it is never overwhelmed or scarce) may not seem to fit with what you see happening. But what you see is not all there is to see. Circumstantial evidence is not light. That context is limited. There is always the larger context, the higher purpose, the unfolding of your (and the world's) next growth in wisdom and love.

Eyes exposed to bright Light, after being in darkness, can become overwhelmed at first. One may feel overexposed when Light illuminates a dark and difficult place. When
Light exposes vulnerability or pain,
this may <u>feel </u>awkward, risky, and uncertain.
But Light doesn't cause pain - it illuminates areas

that require attention and healing. Light enables you to see hidden issues that, when healed/resolved, will empower you.

If you don't trust the wisdom of love, you limit your role in bringing the Light of peace into the world. If you believe you know all there is to know about a concern, you will block the love's Light from working through you. You will block yourself from the Light, darkening the very circumstance for which you seek Light.

Love's Connections Create Harmony:

Harmony is realized when one awakens to Inner Light,
and connects with the same Light in all other beings.
This Light knows the existence of love in each life.
Project this Light into thought; manifest it in connections with all life.
Here is Peace.

A man who trusted love's Light: There was a refugee from the Middle East. He and his parents were immigrants from another country. His circumstances were very difficult (poverty, oppression, prejudice, violence, racism). Based on circumstantial evidence, it appeared he would not overcome his difficulties. He wasn't welcome in the new country. Sadly, he was killed at age 33. But despite his lowly status, he trusted a larger, divine context. His love's Light made a wonderful difference in the country he lived, and in the world.

He didn't hate his oppressors; he loved them. This was his love light shining to all. His name was Jesus. He was strong because he used love's Light to see the world in which he lived. Do you? He said it's best if you do...No exceptions. Remember that the same Light of love is in you. You are not an exception. It's in ALL. Find it, and you find the heart of love. Jesus loved his 'enemies' and treated them with love. He said our love is the only true armor in the world. Be protected in love - love is your shield; and love is your reward.

You have the Power to shine the Light of peace and love into darkness. Do not hide this sacred ability; do not let your concerns take it away. Invest yourself in peace and <u>love</u>, and you will make an everlasting difference to ALL.

The Goals of Relationship:

to Grow in Love, and to Improve All of Life.

Healthy relationships are keys to a healthy life. Healthy relationships provide valuable lessons and experiences such as acceptance, security, support, affection, <u>family</u>, identity, and more. Unhealthy relationships create toxic perceptions and beliefs such as fear, confusion, self-doubt, mistrust, irresponsibility, and blame.

Intention is one of the most important ingredients for healthy relationships. Be sure your intention for all relationships is to grow in <u>love </u>and improve <u>yourself</u>. An intention is a seed.

Plant it in your life's garden. Give it the nourishment and care it needs to grow. Planting it in someone else's garden leaves you <u>dependent</u> on them to care for it. If they don't want it, they will not be motivated to nourish it. Furthermore, they may refuse to acknowledge it was planted at all. Thus, be sure your primary <u>intention</u> is to improve your part in the relationship. If your primary intention is for someone else to improve, experiencing joy and love will be difficult.

Healthy communication tools and relationship skills increase your opportunities for loving connections. In a healthy relationship, you understand what is and is not your responsibility. This brings personal and relational <u>peace.</u> If the other person in the relationship does not want the relationship improved, or is trying to keep it from improving, respect their decision. Let go of any toxic connection. Remember you cannot force another person to be healthy. If you try to force another person into health, you are actually joining them in their dis-ease. You are then at risk of being <u>codependent </u>on his/her decisions. What you try to control controls you.

Improving communication is a marathon, not a sprint. Improved communication happens step by step and is a life-long process. Be patient with yourself and with others.

As <u>communication </u>progresses, relationships have

more opportunities to grow, they take less effort, and they bring more love and joy. When using new ways of communicating and relating, you may feel awkward. With practice, you will be more comfortable and relaxed (even in situations where there is <u>conflict</u>). Misunderstandings and conflicts are typical and resolvable when both people are willing to improve the way they communicate. Be aware when changing your communication style and behaviors, as others may be uncomfortable with this change. They may try to pressure you to revert back to what is familiar to them. Be confident in your new patterns, while being patient and compassionate with other reactions and adjustments.

Communication is the main way people let each other know who they are and how they wish to relate. Desires are stated; responses are delivered. Both messages must be respected, even if disagreeing about statement and/or response. If the person stating the desire believes the responder does not have the right to choose to say "no" or "yes", he/she may focus on trying to control and manipulate the other's response. This is a waste of energy. To be in a healthy relationship, focus away from believing the other person is the problem. Do not blame. Blame makes the situation more difficult. People are not problems. Take time to discern what the actual issue is. Become a part of the solution to the issue. Learn about the other person. Know that the other person is free to choose their own response. It is futile and counterproductive to attempt to force someone to change. It is not your responsibility to change the other person.

You can love another person by what is in *your* heart. If you only 'love' them because they do what you want them to do, this is not genuine love; it is rejection of who they are. Fear tells you that loving them will hurt you if you don't get what you want. But love does not insist on another being different from who they are. Love is accepting; it is unconditional. Acceptance does not mean you agree with the other person's ideas or behaviors. Love can be uncomfortable, but it is not dangerous. Discomfort can signal an opportunity for self-growth.

The degree to which two people accept each other is a major factor in the health of a relationship. You have no right to judge a person as unacceptable. However, you do have a responsibility to admit you are having a difficult time accepting a person. In this awareness, your love evolves. Make your heart and mind a more usable channel for Grace to flow through - this is always beneficial to you!

Love unconditionally. This brings freedom from destructive emotions. When you allow yourself to be upset with someone, sooth yourself with love for that person. Your love is stronger than your pain. This love creates a bridge in a fractured relationship. If both people choose to walk the bridge, healing can occur. Without a bridge of love, healing is not possible.

Accepting another person is related to your ability to accept yourself. The more you are able to accept <u>yourself</u>, your differences, your potentials, and your limitations, the more you are able to accept these in another person. Self-acceptance evolves as you choose to see yourself honestly and realistically, through the honest eyes of Love. Self-acceptance grows as you realize your <u>freedom</u> and responsibility to make your own decisions. As you grow, you realize the other person's freedom and responsibility is their own decision.

With freedom comes responsibility; with responsibility comes freedom. Each person is only responsible for doing their best. It is no one's responsibility to compare whose best is best! <u>Love</u> is not a contest it's constant. You can choose what you want to change about yourself. You can tell the other person what you would like to see them change. It is your responsibility to be honest. The honest expression of yourself is the opportunity for the other to love you.

When both people are being honest and responsible for him/her, both can more easily depend on the other. Make goals together to improve relationship patterns. Set goals which are realistic, concrete, specific, and understood by both people. As goals are developed and action steps are

taken, cooperate to be sure both people
are appreciated, valued, and cared for.

Remember: relationships are for the purpose of growing in your ability to love yourself and the other person. Relationships are NOT for the purpose of getting your way, getting things, or controlling someone. Your happiness in a relationship is directly dependent on your love in the relationship.

Self-Awareness

We are each whole, and a part of the whole. Those who see themselves as whole make no demands. They live life as an expression of their best selves, not as a reaction to others or to the environment. In this way, they are not dependent on the external to define them. Being their best <u>self</u>, for the benefit of all, is the source of their joy.

To have confidence in the self, we must know the self. We can only know the truth about ourselves through eyes of love, not fear. Our precious part of the <u>Divine</u> whole may seem tiny. Yet it holds our part of everything that is Joy and Love. Each of us has all the ingredients we need. We will never be known or loved for anything else.

If you want to feel loved, express yourself to the world around you. You will not feel loved and accepted for what you keep hidden. It is what you honestly <u>expose</u> that can be loved.

When you do not embrace the Divine truth about yourself, you create an *illusion* of who you are. This false sense of self will never seem good enough. The illusion brings with it a burden to push yourself to become someone you were not meant to be.

"Integrity:

Drop the things that offend your soul. Embrace your truth.
It's your life; let no one live it for you."
Wisdom found

In each of us, there are many forms of wisdom. Wisdom impacts our thoughts, emotions, and intuitions. It opens minds, hearts, and senses to reveal the depth of Love. Wisdom creates the ability to soar far beyond what appeared to be troubled times and spaces. By joining all forms of wisdom (both within and between each being), harmony is created. This harmony nurtures peace in each heart, each relationship, and each community.

Knowing Wisdom, we see ourselves as a part of the whole; as all life joined together as the revelation of one, expressed as all.

The ego/mind alone does not have wisdom. Our minds/egos collect facts, ideas, and theories. This information is limited by the context and paradigm of the mind/ego perception. It sees each life as separate (not joined). The ego's goal is survival. It

133

perceives itself as a separate entity from what it needs in order to survive. Thus, the ego believes survival requires acquisition. Whatever the ego believes is needed to increase its chances of survival (physical or emotional), the ego seeks to acquire. It believes its perception is correct, without understanding its limits.

Wisdom provides understanding to go beyond the limits of what is within ego's perception. Ego's only knowledge of the world beyond itself is its ability to trust wisdom. Wisdom sees all as a part of the whole; all as joined together as a revelation of One. Wisdom reveals the non-linear in the linear; the Divine in what is created. Wisdom allows the understanding that existence is the manifestation of Holiness; Holiness creating existence.

The Wisdom of Love illuminates the greatest context. To experience this context is to override ego's logic with Love's Wisdom. This requires each of us to demand our brain focus on Love and possibility; not on fear, hate, and pessimism. This Wisdom knows peace is possible, no matter the ego's perception of problems. It is our responsibility to let Love guide us, rather than using ego's logic as our guide.

Love's Wisdom is more available and powerful than any problem. It has always been with us, creating in and through our lives. It is the reason we made it this far!! When we consciously realize this Wisdom, we more joyfully, confidently, and intentionally create the manifestations of our Love. We are free from judgment, resentment, disgust, and any other aggressive attitude toward others and self. Love's Wisdom is given unlimited power in our minds.

What the scriptures teaches on awareness.

Genesis 3:7

Then the eyes of both of them were opened, and they knew that they were naked; and they sewed fig leaves together and made themselves loin coverings.

Matthew 12:15

But Jesus, aware of this, withdrew from there. Many followed Him, and He healed them all,

John 6:61

But Jesus, conscious that His disciples grumbled at this, said to them, "Does this cause you to stumble?

Luke 24:31

Then their eyes were opened, and they recognized Him; and He vanished from their sight.

Genesis 42:7

When Joseph saw his brothers, he recognized them, but he disguised himself to them and spoke to them harshly. And he said to them, "Where have you come from?" And they said, "From the land of Canaan, to buy food."

Genesis 3:5

"For God knows that in the day you eat from it your eyes will be opened and you will be like God, knowing good and evil."

1 Corinthians 6:19

Or do you not know that your body is a temple of the Holy Spirit who is in you, whom you have from God, and that you are not your own?

Acts 17:28

For in Him we live and move and exist, as even some of your own poets have said, 'For we also are His children.'

Psalm 139:7-8

Where can I go from Your Spirit? Or where can I flee from your presence? If I ascend to heaven, you are there; If I make my bed in Sheol behold, you are there.

Jeremiah 23:24

"Can a man hide himself in hiding places, so I do not see him?" declares the LORD "Do I not fill the heavens and the earth?" declares the LORD.

1 John 1:9

If we confess our sins, He is faithful and righteous to forgive us our sins and to cleanse us from all unrighteousness.

John 1:29

The next day he saw Jesus coming to him and said, "Behold, the Lamb of God who takes away the sin of the world!

John 1:48

Nathanael said to Him, "How do you know me?" Jesus answered and said to him, "Before Philip called you, when you were under the fig tree, I saw you."

John 4:19

The woman said to Him, "Sir, I perceive that you are a prophet.

Ephesians 6:12

For our struggle is not against flesh and blood, but against the rulers, against the powers, against the world forces of this darkness, against the spiritual forces of wickedness in the heavenly places

Proverbs 12:18 "There is one whose rash words are like sword thrusts, but the tongue of the wise brings healing."

"THE BEST DREAMS HAPPEN WHEN WE ARE AWAKE"

Whatever you give life to will live! Whatever you kill has to die!

This is the law of reaping and sowing.

The End

Credits
Some material for this book has been sourced from the following:
W.E.Vines Merrill F Unger & William White, Jr Expository
Dictionary of Biblical Words, copy written 1984 Thomas Nelson,
Inc., Publishing The Broadman Bible Commentary Copy written
1969-Broadman Press, The King James Bible, The Thompson
Chain reference bible copy written 1988, Webster's II New
Riverside Dictionary, Builders Owners and Management Institute
Workbook.   ©

Made in the USA
Columbia, SC
21 October 2021

47114251R00078